FONDUE

BARRON'S

FONDUE

Recipe Photographs: Michael Brauner
Buying Guide and Kitchen
Techniques Photographs: Michael Brauner/Teubner Studio

Recipes:
Petra Casparek   Angelika Ilies
Martina Kittler   Gudrun Ruschitzka

Buying Guide and Kitchen Techniques: Annette Heisch

Contents

RECIPE GUIDE

How cozy it is for host and guests to gather around a pot and cook. Cheese fondue was invented in the Alps in French-speaking Switzerland. Farm families prepared what they had at hand—cheese, wine, and bread—for their evening meal: Cheese was melted in wine. Bread cubes were speared on a fork, dunked, and eaten with gusto. The name *fondue* comes from the French word *fondre*, which means to melt. More than 50 years ago a Swiss gourmet had the idea of adapting cheese fondue to meat. From this experiment was born Fondue Bourguignonne, and the ritual of frying tender pieces of meat in a community pot became a culinary party. Accompanying sauces, dips, and preserves made the gathering complete. Other fondue variations come from Asia, where for hundreds of years it has been a tradition to cook meat, vegetables, and mushrooms in a hot pot in well-seasoned broth. All fondues have one thing in common: Every guest is his own cook. The hosts manage preparation ahead of time and can relax and enjoy their guests.

Fondue: Perfect for Entertaining

A second fondue set is recommended when there are more than six diners.

A fondue is ideal for a pleasant evening with a small group. There should not be more than six persons per pot, or guests cannot comfortably reach the pot with their fork and the pot's capacity is too small. Cheese fondue is a typical fall or winter dish. Meat, vegetables, mushrooms, and fruit can be cooked at any time of the year in a bubbling pot of oil or broth. In summer, it's delightful to serve fondue alfresco.

Shopping and Preparation

Allow at least 5 ounces (150 g) of bread for each person. Place only enough fish or meat on the table for the first portion. Cover remaining platters with foil and refrigerate until they are served.

Prepared sauces and preserves can be purchased well in advance. Homemade chutneys should be prepared two weeks ahead so the flavors blend well. Vegetables, fruit, and mushrooms should be as fresh as possible. It doesn't hurt to purchase cheese a few days ahead, but do not cut it until shortly before melting. Homemade sauces can be prepared a day or so ahead; stir them just before serving. Meat and fish should be freshly purchased, and cubed at the last minute; if you want meat in thin slices, ask the butcher to cut it on a slicing machine. (Be sure to have paper placed between the slices or they will stick together.) The amounts in the recipes are generous, since fondue parties last a few hours and guests may be inclined to indulge.

Setting the Table

Do not cover your table with your best tablecloth; fondue can splash and drip. Use a washable cover or one made of plastic. Washable place mats are also good for the fondue table. Set the table with plates, silverware, and fondue forks, and have plenty of paper napkins ready. Stand the heating element in the middle of the table so that everyone can easily reach the pot. Don't forget the salt shaker and peppermill. Have a shaker of cayenne pepper available, too, for those who like it.

Beverages

The beverages that go with fondue are as varied as the fondue palette itself. Traditionally black tea is drunk with cheese fondue. Chilled white wine is typically poured with fish and vegetable fondues. Cold beer is perfect with an English cheese or spicy meat fondue, and red wine is good with beef or game. Choose light, fruity red wines such as Beaujolais or Valpolicella. Light red wines taste best lightly chilled. And don't forget nonalcoholic drinks such as mineral water and fruit juices.

Hot, unsweetened black tea tastes great with cheese fondue and promotes digestion. A glass of brandy—kirsch, grappa, or Calvados, for example—is also a good choice.

Choosing the Right Recipe

A guide for selecting the right fondue for any occasion is on the next few pages. Each recipe is given color-coded ratings such as "Easy," "Economical," or "Quick to prepare." You will find the color codes repeated on the recipe pages.

Time

Some fondues require a good deal of preliminary slicing and sauce preparation. Others are practically effortless. In the chart you will find preparation and chilling times. All fondues that take 45 minutes or less to prepare are noted as "**Quick**" in the chart. The ones that require lengthy preparation and chilling time are marked "**Takes time**."

Calories

The calorie and fat content per person is listed with each fondue (most are for four servings; some serve six, eight, or more). Fondues containing not more than 400 calories (without bread) are marked "**Low calorie**."

Difficulty of Preparation

Recipes that pose no problem for a beginning cook get the caption "**Easy to prepare**." Only a few fondues in this book are harder; they are marked "**For skilled cooks**."

Other Information

Some fondues have been favorites for decades, and they are labeled "**Classic**."
Variations of fondue are enjoyed in many countries worldwide. Those that originate in specific countries—for example, Japan, China, Italy, or Switzerland—are so listed, as "**Specialty from** ...."
Fondues that are economical to fix, and vegetarian examples, are so noted.

Special Recipes

We have presented a few fondues in the book as "special" recipes, with additional information about optional ingredients and other tips. Each of these special recipes is printed on a yellow page.

RECIPE GUIDE

Page	Recipe	Preparation time	Calories/ serving	Fat/ serving	Low calorie
	WITH BROTH				
36	**Colorful Vegetable Fondue**	45 min.	735	35 g	
37	**Vegetarian Fondue**	1 ¼ hrs.	295	14 g	
38	**Light Fondue with Chicken and Vegetables**	1 hr.	395	6 g	
39	**Spring Fondue with Shitake Mushrooms**	45 min.	320	10 g	
40	**Vegetarian Hot Pot**	1 hr.	565	31 g	
41	**Mushroom Fondue with Beet-Green Rolls**	2 ½ hrs.	310	18 g	
42	**Quick Fish Fondue**	45 min.	505	27 g	
43	**Wine Fondue with Fish**	2 hrs.	720	41 g	
45	**Elegant Fish Fondue**	2 hrs.	495	31 g	
46	**Fish Fondue with Creamy Broth**	1 hr.	445	30 g	
47	**Fish Fondue with Beet-Green Rolls**	1 hr.	205	5 g	
48	**Fish Fondue Canary Island Style**	1 ½ hrs. (+ 2-3 hrs.)	555	32 g	
49	**Japanese Shrimp Pot**	1 hr. (+ 1 hr.)	385	7 g	
50	**Caribbean Coconut Fondue**	1 ¼ hrs.	270	45 g	
51	**Hot Pot with Sushi Rolls**	1 ½ hrs.	230	3 g	
53	**Chinese Fondue**	1 ½ hrs.	785	23 g	
54	**Shabu Shabu**	1 ¼ hrs. (+ 2 hrs.)	640	24 g	
55	**Sukiyaki**	1 hr. (+ 2 hrs.)	765	36 g	
56	**Spicy Thai Fondue**	1 ½ hrs.	570	8 g	
57	**Mongolian Hot Pot**	1 hr.	745	23 g	
58	**Korean Hot Pot**	1 hr. (+ 2 hrs.)	495	19 g	
59	**Roast Beef Fondue**	1 ¼ hrs. (+ 2-3 hrs.)	540	29 g	
60	**Special-Occasion Wine Fondue**	1 ¼ hrs.	690	38 g	
61	**Bollito Misto Fondue**	2 hrs.	785	55 g	
62	**Lamb Fondue**	1 hr. (+ 1 hr.)	555	49 g	
63	**Indian Lamb Fondue**	1 ¼ hrs. (+ 1 hr.)	620	43 g	
64	**Ham Fondue**	45 min.	695	60 g	
65	**Sausage Fondue**	45 min.	605	46 g	

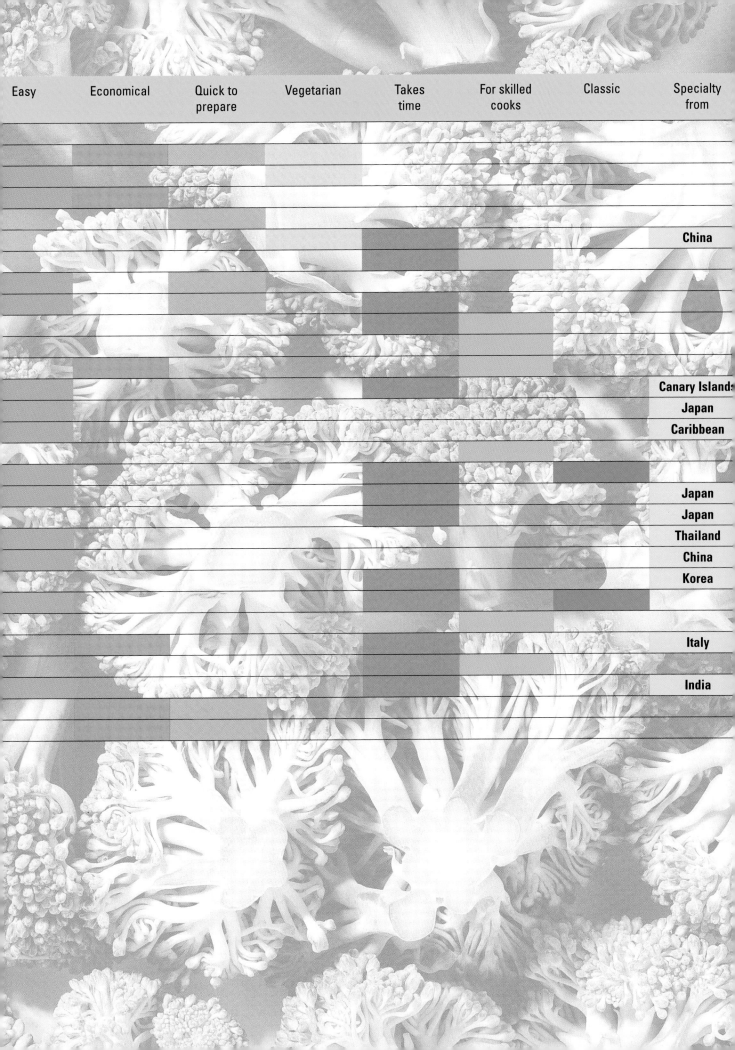

Easy	Economical	Quick to prepare	Vegetarian	Takes time	For skilled cooks	Classic	Specialty from
							China
							Canary Islands
							Japan
							Caribbean
							Japan
							Japan
							Thailand
							China
							Korea
							Italy
							India

RECIPE GUIDE

Page	Recipe	Preparation time	Calories/ serving	Fat/ serving	Low calorie
	WITH OIL				
68	**Fondue Bourguignonne**	2 hrs.	770	60 g	
69	**Mixed Meat Fondue**	1 hr.	720	31 g	
70	**Ground Meat Fondue**	1 hr.	900	62 g	
71	**Potato Fondue**	50 min.	740	53 g	
72	**Colorful Sausage Fondue**	45 min.	765	61 g	
73	**Batter-Crisped Vegetables**	1 hr.	730	57 g	
74	**Bavarian Mushroom Fondue**	2 hrs.	610	20 g	
75	**Bagna Cauda**	1 hr.	785	74 g	
76	**Iltalian Fondue**	1 ¼ hrs.	760	72 g	
77	**Spanish Fondue**	1 hr.	970	77 g	
78	**Mexican Fondue**	1 ¾ hrs.	775	53 g	
79	**Tex-Mex Fondue**	1 hr. (+ 1 hr.)	560	34 g	
80	**Crisp Poultry Fondue**	1 hr.	580	31 g	
81	**Fondue with Spicy Meatballs**	1 ½ hrs. (+ 1 hr.)	815	52 g	
83	**Wild Game Fondue**	2 ½ hrs.	710	35 g	
84	**Falafel Fondue**	1 hr. (+ 1 hr.)	560	38 g	
85	**Moroccan Fondue**	1 ¼ hrs.	705	43 g	
86	**Fondue with Meat Skewers**	1 hr. (+ 2 hrs.)	590	49 g	
87	**Fondue Caribbean Style**	30 min. (+ 1 hr.)	635	35 g	
88	**Fondue with Indonesian Saté Skewers**	30 min. (+ 1 hr.)	575	32 g	
89	**Tempura**	1 hr.	650	46 g	
90	**Fondue with Duck Breast**	1 hr.	665	43 g	
91	**Vietnamese Meatball Fondue**	45 min.	800	65 g	
92	**Fondue with Spring Rolls**	1 ¼ hrs.	425	36 g	▓
93	**Tofu and Tempeh Fondue**	45 min. (+ 1 hr.)	600	41 g	
94	**Fish Fondue**	1 ¼ hrs.	675	50 g	
95	**Fish Stick Fondue**	30 min.	800	62 g	
96	**Seafood Fondue**	30 min. (+ 30 min.)	530	35 g	
97	**Root Vegetable Fondue**	50 min.	470	39 g	
98	**New Year's Eve Fondue**	3 hrs.	375	29 g	▓
99	**Crisp Cheese Fondue**	1 hr. (+ 30 min.)	715	50 g	

Easy	Economical	Quick to prepare	Vegetarian	Takes time	For skilled cooks	Classic	Specialty from
							Spain
							Italy
							Italy
							Spain
							Mexico
							Morocco
							Caribbean
							Indonesia
							Japan
							Vietnam

RECIPE GUIDE

Page	Recipe	Preparation time	Calories/ serving	Fat/ serving	Low calorie
	WITH CHEESE				
102	**Neuchâtel Cheese Fondue**	45 min.	625	35 g	
103	**Farmer's Fondue**	1 hr.	930	67 g	
104	**Geneva Fondue**	1 hr.	970	70 g	
105	**Waadtländer Fondue**	1 hr.	690	33 g	
106	**Fondue with Dutch Cheese**	40 min.	840	50 g	
107	**Cheese Fondue with Mushrooms**	50 min.	660	35 g	
108	**Cheese Fondue with Tomatoes**	1 hr.	685	37 g	
109	**Spicy Cheese Fondue**	45 min.	635	28 g	
110	**Beer Cheese Fondue**	1 hr.	645	32 g	
111	**Quick Bacon and Cheese Fondue**	1 1/4 hrs.	615	30 g	
112	**Mushroom Cheese Fondue**	1 hr.	800	56 g	
113	**Cream Cheese Fondue**	1 hr.	595	39 g	
114	**Gorgonzola Provolone Fondue**	50 min.	795	53 g	
115	**Cheese Tortellini Fondue**	40 min.	830	51 g	
116	**Irish Fondue**	1 hr.	720	42 g	
117	**Dill Fondue**	1 hr.	880	44 g	
118	**Fonduta with Truffles**	1 hr. (+ 4-6 hrs.)	765	59 g	
119	**Goat Cheese Fondue**	30 min. (+ 12 hrs.)	785	53 g	
120	**Blue Cheese Fondue**	30 min.	800	46 g	
121	**Feta Cheese Fondue**	45 min.	730	41 g	
122	**Apple Nut Fondue**	1 hr.	685	36 g	
123	**Chicken Curry Fondue**	1 1/2 hrs.	765	37 g	
	SWEET FONDUES				
126	**Dark Chocolate Fondue**	45 min.	465	28 g	
127	**White Chocolate Fondue**	30 min. (+ 30 min.)	410	24 g	
128	**Cappuccino Fondue**	40 min.	550	32 g	
129	**Chocolate Mint Fondue**	25 min.	475	37 g	
130	**Yogurt Fondue**	40 min.	460	30 g	
131	**Sour Cream Fondue**	50 min. (+ 12 hrs.)	530	25 g	
132	**Apricot Mascarpone Fondue**	45 min.	615	46 g	
133	**Raspberry Fondue**	30 min.	600	40 g	
134	**Vanilla Fondue with Waffles**	45 min.	460	25 g	
135	**Ricotta Fondue**	30 min.	585	35 g	
136	**Wintertime Citrus Fluff Fondue**	30 min.	530	13 g	
137	**Coconut Cream Fondue with Tropical Fruit**	45 min.	545	30 g	
138	**Children's Surprise Fondue**	1 1/2 hrs.	440	19 g	
139	**Doughnut Fondue**	1 hr. (+ 1 1/2 hrs.)	665	37 g	

Easy	Economical	Quick to prepare	Vegetarian	Takes time	For skilled cooks	Classic	Specialty from
							Switzerland
							Switzerland
							Switzerland
							Ireland
							Italy

You don't need much know-how for cooking at the table. You'll need a suitable pot with an appropriate heating element, as well as fondue forks or individual strainers. Other items are determined by the type of fondue, with differences between broth, oil, cheese, and sweet fondues.

The Right Pot

Not every pot is suitable for each type of fondue. Read the information about accessories and operation on the following pages: Broth Fondues, page 16; Oil Fondues, page 18; Cheese Fondues, page 19; and Sweet Fondues, page 20. If you want an all-purpose pot, choose one made of stainless steel or enameled cast iron. Ceramic pots called *caquelons* are made especially for cheese fondues; they are not suitable for broth or oil fondues as they can't stand too much heat. There are special hot pots suitable for broth fondues, particularly Asian specialties such as Shabu Shabu and Sukiyaki. Other than these, there are attractive pots made of heatproof glass that are suitable for broth, cheese, and sweet fondues. As a rule, the capacity of fondue pots ranges between 2 and 2½ quarts (1.8l and 2.5l). Try to get a pot with heatproof handles. Pots for broth and oil fondues should have a splash guard with a device for hanging the forks.

The Heating Element

The heating element is both the stand and the source of heat for the fondue pot. The pot must stand firmly and securely on the heating element as well as on the table. Usually the heating element and the pot are sold as a set, but it is also possible to buy each pot separately. Heating elements can be made of stainless steel, wrought iron, or lacquered metal. There is often a saucer of stainless steel, wood, or stone.

Source of Heat

The heart of every heating element is the burner. There are several types:

Sterno

Sterno is probably the most common source of heat for fondue sets and chafing dishes. It comes in solid form in 2.6- and 7-ounce cans as well as in liquid form. If your unit has a self-contained pan, use the liquid; otherwise, just set the can on the burner.

Regulating the Heat: The flame is regulated by opening and closing the hole(s) on top of the heating element. The wider the opening(s), the more

fuel is burned, making for a hotter flame. High heat is used for oil fondues, medium heat for broth fondues, lower heat for cheese fondues, and the lowest heat for sweet fondues.

Tips

• When purchasing, make sure that the burner is easy to handle.
• Before using the fondue set for the first time, read the use and care booklet.
• Have extra Sterno ready for filling.
• When refilling, remember that the burner will be very hot; let it cool first. Heatproof handles are helpful.
• Relight the burner only when the bottle of Sterno has been removed.

Alcohol Burner

Rarely used today, this type of burner holds a nonflammable glass fiber that is soaked with alcohol. The alcohol burner has an irritating odor and is not as reliable as Sterno. Regulating the heat is done as for Sterno, by opening and closing the holes on the burner.

Electric Burner

These are expensive and relatively scarce, but they have the advantage that they can be regulated exactly and are completely odorless and safe. A burner with a thermostatic control should be heated to 170°F (70°C) for chocolate fondue, 190°F (85°C) for cheese fondue, 226°F (100°C) for broth fondue, and 370°F (180°C) for oil fondue. Electric heat is optimal for oil fondues, as it holds a constant temperature.

Gas Burner

Not often found in stores, these are used with a small gas cartridge. The heat can be exactly regulated.

Fondue Forks

Forks are essential for spearing ingredients and holding them in the pot. As a rule, the forks have two tines. If you mainly prepare cheese fondue, add three-tined forks so the bread does not slide off so easily. The handles should be made of plastic, nonconductive metal or wood. Forks with various-color dots are practical, making it easy for each diner to find his fork without a problem. Have at least one, preferably two forks for each person.

Strainers

For broth fondues, you will need small metal strainers with long handles; finely cut pieces of food like spinach and soft foods like cooked dried mushrooms do not fit comfortably on a fondue fork. The strainers are sold inexpensively in Asian housewares shops and in the housewares section of many department stores. They are the usual accessory for a hot pot.

Fondue Plates

Plates with several sections look attractive and are practical for many fondues, as they allow you to separate the different sauces and accompaniments. Up-to-date models even have a compartment for the fondue fork. Complete fondue sets often include plates, or you can buy them separately. Of course, special plates are not a must; the sauces can also be served in preferably small, individual bowls. Special plates are sold for the bread cubes for cheese fondues; they often go with the ceramic pot.

Lazy Susans and Small Dishes

Some fondue sets are fitted with a rotating ring on which you will find several holders for small bowls. These can be filled with dips, sauces, and accompaniments so that all diners can serve themselves. If you do not have a lazy susan for sauces, be prepared with an assortment of other small dishes or bowls for sauces and dips. It's practical to have sauce bowls arranged on a serving platter that can be passed around easily.

BROTH FONDUES

Cooking in bubbling broth has a long tradition in China, Japan, Korea, and Mongolia. Broth fondues are deliciously aromatic, low in fat and calories, and uncomplicated to prepare.

Accompaniments and Arrangement

The Right Pot

True to the style for the broth fondue is the so-called hot pot or Mongolian hot pot, whose central chimney originally held charcoal to provide the necessary heat. Charcoal pots are still suitable for outdoor cooking. The charcoal is placed in the chimney of the broth-filled hot pot and lighted.

It is quicker when the charcoal is placed on a foil-lined baking sheet and heated ahead of time in an oven preheated to the highest heat. Then, with tongs, place the hot coals in the chimney. Modern hot pots are heated with a heating element and Sterno or electricity. Broth fondues can also be prepared in conventional fondue pots made of stainless steel, enameled cast iron, or heat-proof glass.

Strainers, etc.

For foods that cannot easily be speared on fondue forks, small metal strainers are essential. With these, the foods are held in the broth and removed after cooking. Wooden skewers can also be used to dip foods in the broth.

Tips

• Heat the broth in a pot on top of the stove and pour it hot into the hot pot or fondue pot. Fill pot slightly more than half full. If there is too much broth, it can boil over the edge.
• Fill the chimney of the hot pot with charcoal before adding the broth, or heat with Sterno or an electric heater when the broth is already in the pot.
• Have more hot charcoal ready to add during the meal.

Ingredients and Their Preparation

Meat, fish, seafood, and vegetables are suitable. The food must be thinly sliced because the heat of a broth fondue is not intense.

Meat: Beef or pork fillet, veal scaloppini, chicken or turkey breast, leg of lamb and lamb ribs are all suitable. Meat should be cut into thin, fairly small slices. (Read the shopping tips on page 28.)

Meat will be especially flavorful if marinated ahead of time. See marinade recipes on page 21.

Fish and Seafood: Firm-fleshed fish varieties are suitable (see the shopping information on page 28). Cut fish fillets into thin slices and marinate as desired. (See recipes on page 21.) Shrimp is an ideal seafood choice.

Vegetables: Virtually all vegetables can be used—peppers, zucchini, broccoli, carrots, beets, spinach, cauliflower, and many more. Wash and trim the vegetables, cut into small pieces, and arrange decoratively on a platter. Firm vegetables such as green beans, broccoli, and cauliflower should be lightly blanched beforehand.

Mushrooms: Both fresh and dried varieties are suitable. Fresh white or brown mushrooms, shiitake, oyster mushrooms, and other wild types should be wiped clean with a paper towel. Large ones are halved or quartered. Cut oyster mushrooms into bite-size pieces. Asian dried mushrooms should be covered with boiling water and soaked for 30 minutes, then trimmed of hard stems and cut into smaller pieces if necessary.

Accompaniments: Transparent noodles or rice are appropriate for broth fondue. They can be kept warm in a bowl over low heat or heated in a strainer in the broth.

Table Setting

Each guest places the foods in a strainer, on a fork, or on skewers, dips it into the broth, and cooks it for 1 to 3 minutes. The cooked morsel is eaten with a spicy sauce or dip. Alternatively, several pieces of food can be put into the broth all at once and taken out with strainers or skewers when cooked.

Tips

• With mixed meat and vegetable fondues, begin with the meat; this quickly gives the broth a more intense flavor.
• The broth condenses as it cooks, so more broth must be added during the meal. Prepare plenty of broth, about 3 to 4 quarts (3 to 4l). Keep it hot on the stove.
• Do not add too much food to the broth at once or the temperature will plunge. If the broth stops bubbling, pause and wait until it bubbles again. Cover with a lid to keep it from steaming away.

Using Leftovers

The Broth

At the end of dinner the broth is served as soup in small bowls. Thanks to the variety of food cooked in it, the broth will have acquired a wonderful, complex taste. It can also be flavored as desired with rice wine and soy sauce, and finely cut rice noodles and vegetables can be added to taste. It is traditional to beat an egg, drizzle it into the bubbling broth, and serve the resulting egg-drop soup.

BROTH FONDUES

Meats and Vegetables

When there are leftover meats or vegetables from broth fondues, cover them and refrigerate. Meat can be cut into strips, browned in a skillet and served with gravy or wine cream sauce. Or mix up a quick stir fry with vegetables, meat and/or fish. Vegetables can also be marinated in vinaigrette and served as a salad, or used as the basis for a vegetable casserole.

Basic Recipe for Broths

Homemade broths taste simply great and make every fondue a special pleasure. Canned broth, or even bouillon from cubes or powder, is an alternative if you're in a hurry.

Chicken Broth

For 3 to 4 quarts (3 to 4 l):
1 large or 2 small whole chickens
1 large carrot
1 leek, cleaned
2½ ounces (70 g) celery root, peeled, or 2 stalks celery
2 onions
1 garlic clove
2 teaspoons whole white peppercorns
8 whole allspice berries
2 teaspoons salt
2 bay leaves
3 sprigs fresh thyme
8 parsley stems

Wash chicken and place in a large pot. Add coarsely chopped vegetables, halved peeled onions, garlic, spices, and herbs. Pour in 4 quarts (4 l) cold water, and bring to boil. Cover and simmer over low heat 1½ hours, skimming foam as necessary.

Pour broth through a fine sieve.

Variation

For an Asian fondue, add 1 piece peeled fresh ginger root (about 2 inches [5 cm] long), 1 stem lemongrass, 2 tablespoons rice wine and, if desired, 1 red chili pepper.

Beef Broth

For 3 to 4 quarts (3 to 4 l):
3 pounds (1.3 kg) beef shank, brisket, or short ribs
1½ pounds (700 g) beef bones
3 large onions
2 carrots
4 parsley roots or 1 bunch fresh parsley
2 teaspoons whole black peppercorns
3 bay leaves
2 teaspoons salt

Place meat and bones in a large pot. Add halved onions, peeled carrots, parsley, spices, and salt. Pour in 4 quarts (4 l) cold water. Cover and simmer 3 hours, skimming foam as necessary. Strain broth through a fine sieve.

Fish Broth

For 3 to 4 quarts (3 to 4 l):
3 pounds (1.4 kg) lean fish trimmings without gills (head and bones from sole, turbot, etc.; not salmon, as it is too fatty)
3 leeks, cleaned
1 fresh fennel bulb
2 carrots
2 parsley roots or ½ bunch fresh parsley
3 stalks celery
3 cups (700 ml) dry white wine
4 bay leaves
2 teaspoons whole white peppercorns
2 teaspoons salt

Wash fish under cold running water. Cut leeks into 1-inch (2-cm) pieces. Cut fennel lengthwise into eighths. Peel carrots and parsley roots and quarter lengthwise. Clean and coarsely chop celery.

Combine fish, vegetables, wine, 3 to 4 quarts (3 to 4 l) cold water, bay leaves, pepper, and salt in a large pot and bring to boil. Skim foam, cover, and simmer 2 hours. Strain broth.

Variation

Add 1 tablespoon fennel seeds or 1 to 2 tablespoons dry vermouth to broth.

Vegetable Broth

For 3 to 4 quarts (3 to 4 l):
3 onions, unpeeled
3 garlic cloves, unpeeled
12 ounces (300 g) celery root with leaves, or 1 bunch celery
4 carrots
2 parsley roots or ½ bunch fresh parsley
1 leek, cleaned
2 tablespoons vegetable oil
3 bay leaves
4 whole cloves
2 teaspoons whole black peppercorns
6 whole allspice berries
1 large bunch parsley
3 sprigs fresh thyme
2 teaspoons salt

Quarter onions; halve garlic cloves. Coarsely chop celery, carrots, and parsley roots. Halve leek lengthwise and cut into large pieces.

Heat oil in a large pot. Briefly sauté onion and garlic. Add vegetables and sauté briefly. Add spices, herbs, and salt. Pour in 4 quarts (4 l) water, bring to boil, cover, and simmer over low heat 1½ hours. Strain broth through a sieve. Season to taste with salt.

Tips

• Broth can be prepared in a pressure cooker in half the time. Be sure that the pot is large enough or the broth will boil over. Set temperature at moderate heat.

• Chicken and beef broths should have fat removed. Cool, then chill the broth; lift off the layer of hardened fat with a large spoon. If there's no time for this method, use paper towels to absorb as much fat as possible from the surface of the broth.

• Another possibility is to use a fat-removal pitcher, sold in housewares shops.

• Leftover broth can be frozen for up to three months. Simmer the broth again uncovered to reduce and concentrate it, then freeze in small plastic storage containers.

OIL FONDUES

With the oil fondue, food is fried in hot oil until deliciously crisp. The classic version is Fondue Bourguignonne.

Accompaniments and Arrangement

The Right Pot
Pots of stainless steel, enamel, tinned copper or cast iron are suitable for oil fondues. Do not use a ceramic pot made for cheese fondue; aside from being too shallow, it will crack from the oil's high heat. The pot should narrow at the top so that the hot oil cannot spatter. For the same reason, an attached spatter guard is helpful; the fondue forks can also hang from it conveniently. Read the Source of Heat section on page 15.

Tips
• Fondue pots with a lid are practical because the oil will reheat quickly. If your fondue set does not have a lid, use any other pot lid that fits.
• If you don't have a suitable fondue pot to fit your heating element, use any suitable cooking pot. It is important that the pot sits on the element firmly, without rocking.

Forks
Prepare two-tined fondue forks (see page 21), using at least one per person.

Choosing the Oil
All standard vegetable oils are suitable for high heating; try peanut, corn, canola, mixed vegetable, or grapeseed oil. Clarified butter, though expensive, is also good. Some gourmet shops carry special fondue oils, usually grapeseed oil made fragrant with herbs. The classic Japanese tempura is prepared with clear sesame oil. Expensive cold-pressed oils are not suitable. Neither is butter or margarine, which will cause spattering and burning. For the recipes in this book you will need about 1 quart (1l) of oil.

Tips
• First heat the fat in the fondue pot on the stove.
• The pot should only be filled halfway with fat so that it does not spatter or splash.
• The ideal temperature is 350°F (180°C). To test for the right temperature, hold the handle of a wooden spoon in the oil; small bubbles should form around it.
  Alternatively, dunk a bread cube in the oil; it should brown in less than 1 minute.
• After using the oil, filter it through a sieve lined with a coffee filter or paper towel to remove burned particles. Pour the oil into a container with a tight-fitting lid, seal closed, and store in a dark place.
• Reuse the oil within six to eight weeks for sautéing or frying, or use for other fondues. Do not reheat the oil more than

three times, and discard it if it develops an "off" odor.
• Never pour used oil down the sink. Discard it in a well-sealed container in the household garbage.

Ingredients and Their Preparation

Meat, fish, seafood, vegetables, and mushrooms are suitable for frying in hot oil. Their preparation is similar to that used for broth fondue. The meat for oil fondues is usually cut into cubes, and the vegetables are cut into bite-sized pieces. Marinades and batters vary the results. (See recipes on page 21.)

Important: All the foods for an oil fondue must be patted dry so water drops will not cause spattering when they come in contact with the hot oil.

Table Arrangement
Each guest spears pieces of food on a fondue fork and fries them in the hot oil for one to three minutes. The cooked food is pushed off the fork onto the diner's plate and eaten with suitable sauces.

Tips
• The cooked pieces should be well drained on the rim of the pot or they will be too greasy. It is practical to prepare plates covered with white paper napkins or towels on which the hot foods can be drained briefly. Change the napkins frequently.
• If the oil cools too much to cook food within three minutes, pause and reheat it. Cover it with a lid to speed reheating.
• Never fry in oil that isn't hot enough. The cooked food will be soaked with fat, and meats will toughen.

Using Leftovers
Refrigerate leftover meat and vegetables and sauté or stir-fry in a little oil in a skillet or wok. Serve with or without sauce on noodles or rice.

CHEESE FONDUES

The roots of the original cheese fondue lie in the western Swiss Alps. Cheese is melted in white wine. Diners dunk pieces of bread into the creamy mixture which coats the bread deliciously.

Accompaniments and Arrangement

Cheese fondue is prepared and served in wide, flat pots, also called *caquelons*. They are usually made of ceramics, which heats slowly and evenly. Cheese fondue can also be prepared in a stainless steel or enamel fondue pot, but be sure to keep the heat low enough to keep the cheese from burning. For heat sources, see page 15.

Ingredients and Their Preparation

The Cheese
The choice and combination of cheeses determines the character of the fondue; see page 32 for more on this. Both the variety and the age of the cheese are important.
How much? Count on 6 to 8 ounces (150 to 200 g) cheese for each person.
Cutting: The cheese is cut ahead of time so that it melts easily in the wine. Whether it is coarsely chopped or finely shredded depends on its consistency and age. Young and soft cheeses are coarsely grated or cut into thin slices with the help of a cheese plane or sharp knife. Older and harder

cheese is finely grated. A food processor with a grating disk will save time.

The Wine
The wine should be dry and on the acidic side; the cheese requires acid to bind with the wine. The wines from Switzerland, Neuenberger, Fendant, and Waadtland are traditional favorites; if you can find one of these wines, by all means give it a try. There are also specialty cheese fondues that are prepared with rosé, beer, or apple wine. In each case you should have lemon juice ready. If the wine is not sufficiently acidic, the acid in the lemon juice helps to bind the mixture. Stir in lemon juice by the teaspoon.

Preparation
Rub the inside of the fondue pot with 1 halved clove garlic.

Pour in the wine and warm on top of the stove. Gradually stir in the grated cheese over

low heat; the mixture should never be allowed to bubble. Stir constantly with a wooden spoon.

Stir cornstarch into brandy, then stir this into the melted

cheese mixture to thicken. Season to taste. Place the fondue pot with the hot cheese

mixture on the table, with the heating element set on low heat.

Tips
• If the fondue is too thin, stir in some extra chopped cheese and thicken with a mixture of cold wine and cornstarch.
• If the fondue is too thick, stir in a little more wine.
• If the mixture does not melt smoothly and lumps form, the wine probably lacks acidity. Stir in 1 teaspoon lemon juice.
• Cheese fondue is usually flavored with kirsch (cherry brandy), but grappa, pear brandy, French *marc* or other brandies add their own delicate aromas.

The Bread
Crisp baguettes are a must for cheese fondue. Buy slender loaves and cut the bread into bite-size cubes; each piece should have some crust so it can be speared firmly with the fork. Cut the bread shortly before serving so that it doesn't dry out. Do not cut too much at a time; it's better to offer bread as needed. You will need 5 to 8 ounces (150 to 200 g) per person.

Tips
• Other than classic French bread, hearty varieties such as onion, olive, seeded whole-grain loaves, and earthy farmers' bread are also good.
• Raw or cooked vegetable pieces, red-skinned potatoes, or mushrooms bring variety and can be dunked like bread cubes into the fondue.

Table Arrangement

Each guest spears bread cubes or other foods with a three-tined fork and dunks them into the fondue. The mixture should be stirred with the fork so it remains creamy to the end.

Tips
• The wine and cheese will separate if the fondue is not stirred frequently. If this happens, return the fondue to the stove and reheat gently, stirring constantly; stir in a little lemon juice.
• When the fondue is finished a brown crust will have formed on the bottom of the *caquelon*. Do not let it burn; it's delicious. Simply loosen the crust with a fork.

Using Leftovers

Fondue can be reheated the next day and served over potatoes or vegetables, or as a cheese sauce with pasta.

SWEET FONDUES

Above all, sweet fondues are loved by children. But they can make an unusual dessert for sophisticated diners, too. The principle: Fruit or bits of pastry are dipped into a warm, creamy sauce.

Accompaniments and Arrangement

A shallow ceramic cheese fondue pot, or *caquelon,* is well suited for sweet fondues, which do not tolerate high heat and can burn easily. Use a small pot, for sweet fondues are eaten in smaller quantities than savory ones. Small ceramic fondue pots are offered in specialty shops.

Tips
• To ensure that a chocolate fondue does not burn, prepare it in a heatproof bowl over a hot water bath, then pour into the *caquelon.*

• Before filling the *caquelon,* warm it with hot water.
• If you don't have a *caquelon,* use another heatproof pot with handles—for example, a small soufflé dish.
• Always use low heat to prevent the mixture from burning.

Ingredients and Their Preparation

Chocolate Fondue
The variety of chocolate determines the flavor of the fondue. Children prefer mild varieties—milk chocolate or white chocolate. Adults may prefer the intense, spicy taste of a fine-quality semisweet chocolate. Chop the chocolate coarsely. Combine with milk or cream, and melt over low heat, stirring constantly. Add rum, orange liqueur, or cognac for flavor and aroma.

Other Sweet Fondues
Dairy products such as yogurt, cottage cheese, crème fraîche, mascarpone, and cream are good bases for sweet fondues. Lemon, orange or lime peel is a good addition. These fondues are frequently thickened with cornstarch: Stir it into cold liquid, then mix into the fondue and heat.

Fruits for Dunking:
Fruit should be fresh, ripe, but still crisp and firm. All fruits must be cut into bite-size

pieces. Allow 5 to 8 ounces (150 to 200 g) per person.
Pears, Apples: Wash, dry, quarter, remove core, and cut fruit into bite-size pieces. Toss or sprinkle with lemon juice to prevent browning.
Bananas: Peel, slice, and sprinkle with lemon juice.
Plums, Peaches, Apricots: Wash, dry, halve, remove pits, and cut into bite-size pieces.
Cherries, Grapes, Strawberries: Wash and pat dry. Halve large strawberries if necessary.
Tangerines, Oranges: Peel and slice or section. Carefully remove all white membrane.
Figs: Wash, wipe dry, and quarter.
Kiwis: Peel and cut into wedges.
Mango: Peel; cut the flesh from the pit in slices. Cut into bite-size pieces.

Papaya: Peel, halve, remove seeds, and cut fresh into bite-size pieces. Sprinkle with a little lime or lemon juice.

Pastries and Cakes:
Ladyfingers, gingerbread, yeast coffeecake, pound cake, cookies, raisin bread, and small doughnuts are all good for dunking. Cut into bite-size pieces and arrange on plates.

Tips
• For a sweet fondue that doesn't involve chocolate or a creamy sauce, dip fruit pieces into a batter (see recipes on page 21) and fry them in hot oil

in a fondue pot until crisp and browned. Drain, sprinkle with cinnamon sugar, and serve hot.
• Sweet fondues are a good opportunity to use leftover cake and pastries.
• If you want less sweetness, dip cubes of baguette or nut bread into chocolate fondue.
• Marshmallows dipped in chocolate fondue make a hit for children's birthday parties.

Table Arrangement

Everyone spears fruit, cake cubes, etc., on fondue forks and dips them into the fondue mixture.

Using Leftovers

Remaining prepared fruit such as apples, pears, and cherries can be used in a fruit salad. Sprinkle with a little lemon juice; sweeten with sugar, honey, or maple syrup; and flavor with liqueur if desired. Sprinkle with chopped nuts. Leftover peaches, strawberries, mangos, papayas or apricots can be pureed into a delicate fruit sauce: Sweeten lightly, flavor with a bit of liqueur if you wish, and serve with ice cream or sorbet. Chilled, hardened chocolate fondue can be remelted over a water bath and used as a glaze for cake. Yogurt fondue leftovers can be pureed with milk and fruit into a shake.

Marinades give meat and fish lots of extra flavor. The recipes on this page make enough for about 1³⁄₄ pounds (800 g) meat or fish. For maximum impact, marinate for at least one or two hours. Before preparation, drain the fish or meat and pat dry with paper towels.

Marinades for Meat

Asian

Stir together ¼ cup (2 ounces/ 60 ml) soy sauce, 1 tablespoon rice wine, 2 tablespoons vegetable oil, 1 tablespoon honey, 2 teaspoons grated fresh

ginger, 1 pressed garlic clove, and a pinch of cayenne pepper. Use with poultry or pork.

Caribbean

Stir together 3 tablespoons lime juice, ½ teaspoon grated lime rind, ¼ cup (2 ounces/ 60 ml) vegetable oil, 1 pressed garlic clove, 2 crushed allspice berries, and ½ teaspoon chili powder.
Use with poultry.

Italian

Stir 5 tablespoons basil-flavored olive oil (purchased or homemade), 4 crushed white peppercorns, and 1 tablespoon lemon juice.
Use with beef, veal, or poultry.

Tip

For an especially rich taste, simply sprinkle the meat with 2 to 3 tablespoons truffle oil and a few crushed white peppercorns. The taste of truffles harmonizes well with beef or veal fillet.

Marinades for Fish

French

Stir together 3 tablespoons lemon juice, 2 tablespoons dry white wine, 1 tablespoon grapeseed oil, and 1 teaspoon crushed fennel seeds. Grate in ½ teaspoon lemon rind. (Before grating, try pressing a piece of waxed paper onto the grater until the grates press through. You'll find the lemon rind stays on the paper and is easily scraped off.)

Asian

Stir together ¼ cup (2 ounces/60 ml) lime juice, ½ stick coarsely chopped lemongrass, 1 pressed garlic clove, 1 teaspoon freshly grated ginger root, and ¼ teaspoon chili powder. Remove lemongrass after marinating.

Batters

The amounts given will make a batter for about 1³⁄₄ pounds (800 g) vegetables, fruit, meat, or fish.

Basic Recipe

1 egg, separated
2 cups (8 ounces/200 g) all-purpose flour
1 tablespoon cornstarch
Salt
Pepper
1 cup (250 ml) cold water

Blend egg yolk, flour, cornstarch, salt, pepper, and water into a smooth batter. Let rest 30 minutes; stir. Beat egg whites until stiff and fold into batter. Divide the batter into individual small bowls, one for each guest. Diners spear vegetable pieces, meat, or fish on a fork, dip lightly in the batter, and cook in hot oil until crisp, 2 to 4 minutes.

Variations

Beer Batter: Substitute beer for water. Use with fish and pork.
Wine Batter: Substitute ½ cup (125 ml) dry white wine for water. Use with poultry and vegetables.
Herb Batter: Add finely chopped fresh herbs (parsley, chives, and/or dill) to basic batter or wine batter recipe. Use with fish and vegetables.
Cheese Batter: Mix 2 tablespoons grated hard cheese (such as Gruyère) into basic, wine, or beer batter. Use with poultry and vegetables.
Spice Batter: Season the basic recipe with ¼ teaspoon chili powder and ½ teaspoon each cumin and turmeric. Use with vegetables.
Sweet Batter: Combine 1 cup (4 ounces/125 g) all-purpose flour, ½ cup (125 ml) water or wine, 2 egg yolks, a pinch of salt, ½ teaspoon grated lemon rind, and ½ teaspoon vanilla. Let stand 10 minutes. Beat 2 egg whites until stiff and fold in. Use with fresh fruit.

Tips

• Just before dipping, dust foods with a little flour to help batter cling. (Provide each guest with a small bowl of flour for this purpose.)
• Remove bits of cooked batter from oil frequently with a fine-meshed sieve or skimming spoon; otherwise they will burn and produce an unpleasant taste and smell.
• Have plates lined with paper towels or white paper napkins on the table so diners can drain cooked foods of excess oil.

One plate for each two people is enough, if paper is changed as needed.
• Excellent pancakes can be made from any leftover batter.

SAUCES AND DIPS

Almost all broth and oil fondues depend on sauces to become really delicious meals. Have an interesting assortment of sauces on the table so that there is something for every taste. The recipes on the following pages serve four people. A good rule of thumb: Prepare as many sauces as there will be diners. If you want to offer even more sauces, halve the recipe ingredients.

Classics

These sauces have pampered palates for generations and are always a hit.

Béarnaise Sauce

2 shallots
7 white peppercorns
3 sprigs fresh tarragon
5 tablespoons dry white wine
3 tablespoons white wine vinegar
3 egg yolks
Salt
Pepper
1 stick (4 ounces/125g) cold butter

Peel shallots and dice finely. Crush peppercorns coarsely in a mortar. Finely chop tarragon. Bring wine, vinegar, shallots, pepper, and $2/3$ of the tarragon to boil and cook uncovered until

reduced to $1/4$ cup (60ml). Let cool.

Strain wine mixture into yolks in heatproof bowl or top of double boiler.

Season with salt and whisk over hot water until foamy and creamy. Whisk in butter bit by bit.

Stir remaining tarragon into sauce and season with salt and ground pepper. Serve sauce warm and as soon as possible.

This is perfect with a classic meat fondue such as Fondue Bourguignonne, fish fondue, and fondues with delicate vegetables such as artichokes.

Tip
Many classic sauces are prepared with raw egg yolks, so it is important that the eggs are very fresh.

Variation
Maltese Sauce: Add 1 tablespoon freshly squeezed blood orange juice to the

cooked wine mixture. Stir another tablespoon of blood orange juice and the finely grated rind of $1/2$ orange into the finished sauce.

Variation
Hollandaise Sauce: Over low heat, melt 7 ounces (200g) butter in a small saucepan; do not brown. Skim off foam that rises to top. Beat 3 egg yolks well with 3 tablespoons white wine or water in a stainless steel bowl, then place over a hot water bath. Slowly whisk in butter, at first drop by drop, then in a thin stream until a thick sauce forms. Season with salt, pepper, and lemon juice. Use with fish, poultry, and delicate vegetables such as asparagus.

Tip
You can make the sauce more aromatic by adding a bit of anisette, more lemon juice and rind, or blood orange juice instead of water and grated orange rind.

Tartar Sauce

1 egg yolk
1 teaspoon sharp prepared mustard
Salt
Pepper

$1/2$ teaspoon lemon juice
$1/2$ cup (4 ounces/125ml) vegetable oil
$1/2$ small onion
1 hard-cooked egg
2 small pickled gherkins
1 tablespoon drained capers

Whisk egg yolk with mustard, salt, pepper, and lemon juice. Whisk in 2 tablespoons of the oil drop by drop; then whisk in remaining oil in a thin stream. Beat with the whisk attachment of an electric hand beater until the consistency of thick mayonnaise. Finely chop onion, hard-cooked egg, and gherkins. Add with capers to the sauce.

Use with all meat and fish fondues, as well as broth fondues and oil fondues.

Tip
To save time, use purchased mayonnaise and mix in mustard, onion, egg, gherkins, and capers.

Variations
Mayonnaise made with hard-cooked eggs: Mash 2 hard-cooked egg yolks with a fork. Mix with 2 tablespoons hot water, adding mustard and lemon juice to taste. Gradually whisk in $1/2$ cup (125ml) oil to form a thick, flowing sauce. Season with salt, pepper, and, if desired, some cayenne pepper. Adjust seasoning with mustard and lemon juice.

Tip
This sauce can be the base for different mayonnaise dips. Mayonnaise made with raw egg yolks poses a slight risk of salmonella contamination, but using hard-cooked yolks eliminates this risk. Feel free to prepare the sauce a day ahead and refrigerate.

Mustard Sauce with Dill

1 bunch fresh dill
$1/4$ cup (2 ounces/60ml) mildly sharp prepared mustard
2 tablespoons white wine vinegar
1 teaspoon sugar
10 tablespoons vegetable oil

Finely chop dill. Mix mustard with vinegar and sugar. Gradually whisk in oil. Stir in dill. Use with fish fondues, especially with salmon.

SAUCES AND DIPS

Herbed Egg Sauce

3 hard-cooked eggs
1 teaspoon sharp prepared mustard
1 tablespoon white wine vinegar
6 tablespoons corn oil
1 small pickled gherkin
2 tablespoons chopped fresh herbs (chives, parsley, chervil)
Salt
Pepper

Shell eggs and separate whites from yolks. Mash egg yolks and stir in mustard, vinegar, and oil until creamy. Finely chop gherkin and egg whites and stir with herbs into the yolk mixture. Season to taste with salt and pepper. Use with fish fondue or with vegetable fondue that includes delicate vegetables such as asparagus or artichokes.

Tip

This sauce is sometimes called Sauce Gribiche.

Apple-Horseradish Sauce

1 small sour apple
2 tablespoons lemon juice
1 tablespoon grated horseradish (fresh or bottled)
5 ounces (125 g) crème fraîche
Salt
Pepper
Pinch of sugar
1 tablespoon finely chopped walnuts

Peel and finely grate apple; immediately sprinkle with lemon juice. Mix apple and horseradish into crème fraîche. Season to taste with salt, pepper, and sugar. Fold in walnuts. Use with meat and fish fondues.

Tip

As desired, fold in 1 tablespoon whole cranberry or lingonberry sauce.

Variation

Horseradish Cream: Whip 1 cup (8 ounces/200 g) heavy cream until stiff. Fold in 3 to 4 tablespoons grated bottled horseradish and season with salt, a pinch of sugar, and a little lemon juice if necessary.

International Specialties

Here's a sampling of flavorful sauces from Southern Europe, Asia, and the Americas.

Argentinian Chimichurri

2 small red onions
2 fresh red chili peppers
1 large garlic clove
1/2 bunch parsley
3 tablespoons red wine vinegar
3 tablespoons mild olive oil
1 teaspoon dried oregano
1/4 cup (2 ounces/60 ml) lemon juice
Salt
Pepper

Finely chop onions. Seed and finely chop chilies.

Mince garlic. Finely chop parsley leaves. Whisk vinegar with oil. Fold in onions, chilies, garlic, parsley, oregano, and lemon juice. Season to taste with salt and pepper. Let stand at least 2 to 3 hours at room temperature to develop full flavor. Use with poultry or beef fondues.

Guacamole

2 large very ripe avocados
1/4 cup (2 ounces/60 ml) lemon juice
Salt
Pepper
1/4 teaspoon cayenne pepper
2 garlic cloves
2 green onions
2 tablespoons olive oil

Halve avocados lengthwise and remove seed. Scoop out the pulp with a spoon and mash with a fork. Mix with lemon juice. Season well with salt, pepper, and cayenne pepper. Peel garlic and force through a press into mashed avocado. Cut the green onions into very fine strips. Mix half of the strips into the avocado with the oil. Serve sprinkled with remaining green onion strips. Use with meat fondues.

Tips

• The guacamole will be milder and creamier if you add 2 tablespoons crème fraîche.
• Guacamole tastes best when fresh. Prepare it no more than 1 hour before the meal. Cover and refrigerate.

Indonesian Peanut Sauce

4 ounces (100 g) unsalted peanuts
3 shallots
3 garlic cloves
1 teaspoon sambal oelek (sold in Asian markets)
3 tablespoons peanut oil
2 tablespoons soy sauce
1 tablespoon palm sugar or brown sugar
1 ounce (30 g) firm coconut cream (sold in Asian markets), finely chopped
1 cup (8 ounces/200 ml) chicken broth
2 tablespoons lemon juice
Salt
Pepper

Grind the peanuts moderately fine. Finely dice shallots. Finely chop garlic. Pound shallots,

garlic, and sambal oelek to a paste in a mortar.

Heat oil in a skillet and sauté shallot mixture in it for 1 minute. Add peanuts, soy sauce, sugar, and coconut cream. Pour in broth and lemon juice. Simmer, stirring, for 5 minutes. Season to taste with salt and pepper. Use with meat and vegetable fondues.

Tip

• Peanut sauce is good warm or cold.
• If you don't have time to prepare it, buy bottled peanut sauce, also called saté sauce, in Asian markets.

SAUCES AND DIPS

Aïoli

4 garlic cloves
1/4 teaspoon salt
1/2 tablespoon lemon juice
2 fresh egg yolks
2/3 cup (5 ounces/150ml) extra virgin olive oil

Peel garlic and crush with salt and lemon juice in a mortar. Stir in egg yolks. Place mixture in a bowl and whisk in oil, first drop by drop and then in a thin stream. Use with fish fondue or fondues with delicate vegetables.

Tip

To save time, use 1 cup (8 ounces/250g) purchased mayonnaise and season with 3 to 4 garlic cloves, forced through a garlic press.

Middle Eastern Sesame Dip

2 tablespoons unshelled sesame seeds
1 piece fresh ginger (1/2 inch/1cm long)
5 tablespoons soy sauce
1 teaspoon sesame oil
2 tablespoons lemon juice
1 tablespoon honey
Pinch of cayenne pepper
Salt
Pepper

Toast sesame seeds in a dry skillet over moderate heat until fragrant. Peel ginger and grate finely. Mix sesame seeds and ginger with soy sauce, oil, lemon juice, and honey. Season to taste with cayenne pepper, salt, and pepper. Use with poultry fondue.

Light Dips

Cottage cheese and yogurt are the ideal basis for creamy but relatively low-calorie dips.

Cottage Cheese Cucumber Dip

1 small russet potato, cooked until mealy
5 ounces (150g) cottage cheese
2 tablespoons vegetable oil
1/4 cucumber
about 1 tablespoon each finely chopped fresh chives and dill
1 teaspoon sharp prepared mustard
1 tablespoon lemon juice
Salt
Pepper

Peel potato and mash. Whisk cottage cheese and oil. Peel cucumber and grate into fine shreds. Mix potato, cheese mixture, cucumber, and herbs; season with mustard, lemon juice, salt, and pepper. Use with all meat fondues.

Yogurt Dip

2 ripe tomatoes
About 2 sprigs each fresh basil and fresh mint
2 ounces (50g) mozzarella (preferably buffalo mozzarella)
1/2 garlic clove
1/2 cup (4 ounces/100g) whole-milk plain yogurt
Grated rind of 1/2 lemon
Salt
Pepper

Dip tomatoes into boiling water a few seconds and peel off skin. Core, seed, and dice.

Cut herbs into fine strips. Finely dice mozzarella. Press garlic. Mix tomatoes, herbs, mozzarella, and garlic with yogurt and lemon rind. Season to taste with salt and pepper. Use with meat fondues.

Quick Sauces

With some imagination, tasty sauces can be made of purchased mayonnaise and ketchup in a flash.

Quick Cocktail Sauce

1/2 cup (4 ounces/125g) mayonnaise
5 tablespoons ketchup
1 teaspoon lemon juice
2 drops Tabasco
1 tablespoon orange liqueur (optional)
Salt
Pepper

Mix mayonnaise with ketchup, lemon juice, Tabasco, and, if desired, the liqueur. Season to taste with salt and pepper. Use with meat or seafood fondues.

Thousand Island Dressing

1/2 red bell pepper, seeded
1 small pickled gherkin
1/2 cup (4 ounces/125g) mayonnaise
3 tablespoons ketchup
1/2 teaspoon sweet paprika
Pinch of cayenne pepper
Salt
Pepper

Finely chop red pepper and gherkin. Mix into mayonnaise and ketchup. Season to taste with paprika, cayenne pepper, salt, and pepper. Use with meat fondues.

Olive Dip

5 black olives, pitted
2 anchovy fillets
2 pickled red peppers
6 tablespoons mayonnaise

Finely chop olives with anchovies and peppers. Mix with mayonnaise. Use with vegetable fondues.

Variation: Use green olives instead of black olives. Add 1 teaspoon each finely chopped drained capers and minced parsley.

Curry Dip

1/2 sour apple, peeled
1/2 onion
1/2 cup (4 ounces/125g) mayonnaise
2 teaspoons mild curry powder

Grate apple and finely chop onion. Mix both with mayonnaise and curry powder. Use with meat and fish fondues.

FLAVORFUL GARNISHES

Discriminating diners treasure homemade pickles and preserved vegetables. Here you will find a few really good recipes.

Marinated Vegetables

Peppers in Olive Oil

4 servings
2 each red and yellow bell peppers
½ garlic clove
1 tablespoon lemon juice
2 tablespoons olive oil
Salt
Pepper
1 teaspoon chopped fresh dill

Halve and seed peppers. Roast under broiler or bake at 450°F (250°C) until skin blisters. Let peppers cool, covered with a damp cloth. Finely chop garlic. Whisk lemon juice, oil, garlic, salt, and pepper. Peel peppers and cut lengthwise into strips. Place on a platter and sprinkle with marinade. Cover and refrigerate at least 5 hours. Just before serving, sprinkle with dill. Use with meat and cheese fondues.

Thyme Mushrooms

4 servings
1 pound (400g) small mushrooms
3 green onions
1 large garlic clove
¼ cup (60ml) olive oil
1 teaspoon fresh thyme leaves or ½ teaspoon dried thyme
Salt
Pepper
½ cup (4 ounces/125ml) dry white wine

Wipe mushrooms clean. Cut green onions into rings. Finely chop garlic. Heat oil and sauté mushrooms 2 minutes. Add garlic and onion and sauté briefly. Season with thyme, salt, and pepper. Pour in wine and boil 3 minutes. Let cool. Cover and refrigerate at least 2 hours. Use with lamb fondues.

Tip
Just before serving, sprinkle with a little truffle oil.

Shallots in Balsamic Vinegar

6 servings
12 ounces (300g) small shallots
5 tablespoons olive oil
1 tablespoon sugar
¼ cup (2 ounces/60ml) balsamic vinegar
Salt
Pepper

Peel shallots. Heat oil and sauté shallots. Sprinkle with sugar. Pour in balsamic vinegar and boil briefly, then braise shallots for 4 minutes. Season with salt and pepper. Serve lukewarm or cold. Use with Italian-style cheese and meat fondues.

Zucchini with Ginger

6 servings
1 pound (400g) small zucchini
2 garlic cloves
1 piece (1 inch/2cm) fresh ginger
3 tablespoons vegetable oil
3 coriander seeds, crushed

¼ teaspoon chili powder
½ teaspoon ground cumin
1 teaspoon garam masala (Indian spice mixture)
¼ cup (2 ounces/50g) light brown sugar
¼ cup (2 ounces/50ml) malt vinegar
Salt
Pepper

Cut zucchini into thin slices. Finely chop garlic and ginger. Heat oil, add zucchini, and sauté briefly. Add garlic, ginger, and spices. Sprinkle with sugar, then pour in vinegar and simmer 5 minutes. Season with salt and pepper. Let cool and marinate at least 3 hours. Use with Asian meat fondues.

Tip
When zucchini are large, they should be seeded before cutting. For this, halve zucchini lengthwise and scoop out seeds with a spoon.

Sweet and Sour Preserved Vegetables

Beets with Horseradish

Makes 2 jars, about 12 ounces (350ml) each
1 pound 2 ounces (500g) red beets
1 piece fresh horseradish (1¼ inch/3cm long)
1¼ cups (10 ounces/300ml) red wine vinegar
¼ cup (2 ounces/50ml) water
3 tablespoons light brown sugar
1 teaspoon whole white peppercorns
5 whole cloves
1 bay leaf
½ teaspoon salt

Cover beets with water, and simmer 45 minutes. Drain and

rinse with cold water. Peel beets and cut into ½-inch (1-cm) cubes. Peel the horseradish with a vegetable peeler.

Cut it into thin slices. Layer the warm beets and horseradish in 2 glass jars. Bring vinegar, water, sugar, spices, and salt to boil and pour over beets while hot. Quickly cap with twist-off lids and seal jars. Let beets marinate at least 2 days. In the refrigerator they will keep about 4 weeks. Use with beef fondues.

FLAVORFUL GARNISHES

Piccalilli

8 servings (1 pint/500 ml)
4 ounces (100 g) cucumber
1 red bell pepper
4 ounces (100 g) zucchini
4 ounces (100 g) peeled yellow squash
2 tablespoons salt
1 piece fresh ginger (½ inch/1 cm)
1 teaspoon curry powder
½ teaspoon dry mustard
2 tablespoons sugar
1 cup (8 ounces/225 ml) white wine vinegar
1 onion
1 teaspoon cornstarch

Cut vegetables into ½-inch (1-cm) pieces. Mix with salt and refrigerate overnight. Rinse, then drain well in a sieve. Peel ginger and grate finely. In a pot, mix ginger, curry powder, dry mustard, and sugar; stir in vinegar and bring to boil.

Add vegetables and simmer 10 minutes. Drain in a sieve set over a bowl. Spoon hot vegetables into 1-pint (500-ml) jar and return liquid to the pot. Finely chop onion. Add to marinating liquid and simmer 2 minutes. Mix cornstarch with 1 tablespoon water, stir into hot liquid and bring to boil. Cover vegetables with the hot liquid. Close jar with a twist-off lid and let stand at least 2 days. Piccalilli will keep in the refrigerator for 4 weeks. Use with meat fondues.

Preserved Fruits

Preserved small fruits are not only a visual highlight at the fondue table but also bring a new taste experience.

Spicy Mustard Fruit

6 servings (20 ounces/580 ml)
1 lemon
8 ounces (200 g) sour apples (greening or Granny Smith)
9 ounces (250 g) hard pears (Bosc or Seckel)
2 tablespoons lemon juice
1 tablespoon golden raisins
2 ounces (50 g) dried apricots
½ cup (4 ounces/125 ml) white wine vinegar
½ cup (4 ounces/125 ml) dry white wine
1 cup (8 ounces/200 g) superfine sugar
5 whole cloves
5 coriander seeds
5 whole white peppercorns
½ cinnamon stick
½ teaspoon yellow mustard seeds

Halve lemon lengthwise and cut into thin slices. Peel apples and pears, quarter lengthwise, and remove cores. Sprinkle with lemon juice.

Rinse and drain raisins. Halve dried apricots. Bring vinegar, wine, and sugar to boil; simmer uncovered 5 minutes. Add apples and pears and simmer another 3 minutes. Add raisins and apricots and simmer 1 minute. Transfer fruit with liquid to a glass jar with twist-off lid. Cover and marinate at least 2 days. The mustard fruits can be kept in the refrigerator for 4 to 6 weeks.

Use with meat, poultry, or game fondues.

This is a standard garnish for Bollito-Misto Fondue (page 61).

Mustard fruits get an unusual twist with kiwi, pineapple, and mango.

Piquant Pineapple with Red Peppercorns

8 servings (1½ pints/750 ml)
1 pineapple, about 2¼ pounds (1 kg)
1 orange
1 scant cup (7 ounces/200 ml) raspberry vinegar
¼ cup (2 ounces/50 g) sugar
1 tablespoon whole red peppercorns
2 star anise
5 whole allspice

Quarter pineapple and remove core. Peel fruit, removing

"eyes," and cut into pieces. Reserve juice.

Wash and dry orange; cut off peel in a long spiral. Squeeze juice. Bring vinegar, sugar, orange peel, and spices to boil. Add pineapple with its juice and orange juice and simmer uncovered for 10 minutes. Spoon into jar and seal at once with twist-off lid. This will keep in the refrigerator for 4 to 6 weeks. Use with Asian-style poultry fondues.

Chutneys

These sweet-sour mixtures of fruit, vegetables, onions, and spices are perfect with meat fondues. Chutneys taste best after they have marinated in sealed jars for 1 to 2 weeks. It is most practical to store the chutney in small jars with twist-off lids. Unopened, they will keep for about 3 months. The opened jars will keep in the refrigerator about 4 weeks.

Apple Chutney

4 jars (4 ounces/125 ml each)
1 pound 2 ounces (500 g) sour apples
2 red onions
1 piece fresh ginger root (1/2 inch/1 cm)
2 ounces (50 g) golden raisins
1/2 teaspoon salt
Pinch of cayenne pepper
2 teaspoons crushed yellow mustard seeds
1/2 cup (4 ounces/125 ml) white wine vinegar
1/2 cup (4 ounces/100 g) light brown sugar

Peel apples, quarter, and remove cores. Cut quarters into thin slices. Finely chop onions. Peel ginger and grate coarsely. Mix apples, onions, and ginger with raisins in a saucepan. Stir in salt, cayenne pepper, mustard seeds, vinegar, and sugar and bring to boil. Simmer, stirring occasionally, 35 minutes. Spoon into jars and seal immediately. Use with pork fondues.

Plum Chutney

2 jars (5 ounces/150 ml each)
1 pound 2 ounces (500 g) plums
2 tablespoons red wine vinegar
1/4 cup (2 ounces/65 g) light brown sugar
1 teaspoon crushed whole allspice berries
1 bay leaf
1 whole clove
Salt
Pepper

Halve plums, remove pits, and chop coarsely. In a saucepan, bring vinegar, sugar, and spices to boil. Add plums. Cover and simmer over low heat 40 minutes, then uncover and simmer 5 minutes more. Spoon chutney into jars with twist-off lids and seal immediately. Use with lamb fondue.

Pepper Chutney

4 jars (4 ounces/125 ml each)
2 tomatoes
1 each green and red bell pepper
1 red chili pepper
3 white onions
2 garlic cloves
1/2 teaspoon sweet paprika
Pinch of ground cardamom
6 tablespoons white wine vinegar
5 tablespoons sugar
1/4 teaspoon salt

Dip tomatoes into boiling water to loosen skins; peel, seed, and dice. Halve peppers, seed, and cut into strips. Seed chili pepper and cut into very thin strips. Finely chop onions and garlic. Combine tomatoes, peppers, chili pepper, onions, and garlic with paprika, cardamom, vinegar, sugar, and salt in a saucepan and bring to boil. Simmer, stirring occasionally 50 minutes. Spoon into jars with twist-off lids and seal immediately. Use with all meat fondues.

Orange Chutney

2 jars (4 ounces/125 ml each)
2 oranges
11 ounces (300 g) red onions
1 tablespoon vegetable oil
1 teaspoon fennel seeds
2 tablespoons honey
1/4 cup (2 ounces/60 ml) lime or lemon juice
Salt
Pepper

Finely grate the rind of one orange. Remove white membrane and finely chop the flesh. Squeeze juice of the second orange. Halve onions lengthwise and cut into thin slices. Heat oil and sauté fennel seeds in it briefly. Add onion and sauté briefly. Add orange juice, rind, orange flesh, honey, lime or lemon juice, salt, and pepper and simmer 35 minutes. Spoon into jars with twist-off lids and seal immediately. Use with poultry fondue, especially with duck breast.

Onion Relish

2 jars (12 ounces/375 ml each)
2 pounds (900 g) red onions
1 orange
1 lemon
1 generous cup (9 ounces/250 g) brown sugar
Salt
1 generous cup (9 ounces/250 ml) red wine vinegar
Pinch of cinnamon
1 teaspoon curry powder
1/2 teaspoon dry mustard

Mince onions. Peel orange and lemon and cut flesh into small cubes, removing seeds. Combine onions, orange, lemon, sugar, salt, vinegar, and spices in a saucepan and bring to boil. Cover and simmer over low to medium heat about 1 hour or until thick. Spoon into jars with twist-off lids and seal immediately. Use with poultry, fish, and ground meat fondues.

Tips

• Relishes originated in England; chutneys are from Indian cuisine. Relishes have ingredients that are more finely chopped than chutney. They also have fewer ingredients. The classics are prepared with equal parts of onions and cucumbers or onions and fruits, such as fresh currants. For 2 1/4 pounds (1 kilogram) of vegetables or fruit, you would need 1 generous cup (9 ounces/250 g) sugar and about 1 cup (7 to 8 ounces/200 to 250 ml) vinegar.
• Relishes and chutneys keep well, sealed, for 6 to 12 months.

BUYING GUIDE

With fondue, a simple pleasure, the optimum quality of the ingredients is really important. Here you will find out how to choose the best fish, meat, cheese, and vegetables. There are also many other tips on the numerous ingredients that give fondues their flavor. The fondue pot plays the main role, but piquant additions are essential too. A variety of preserved vegetables, creamy sauces, and subtle chutneys will bring excitement to your fondue table.

Meat

Those who want to be certain of getting the best-quality meat should shop at a natural food store's butcher counter or look for a butcher who can give you information on where the meat comes from. Whatever meat you decide on, for fondue it should always contain a minimum of fat and sinew. The meat is sliced across the grain. Frozen meat should be thawed in the refrigerator. Meat for an oil fondue must be patted thoroughly dry with paper towels or they will spatter when they come in contact with the oil. **Beef** is the classic for meat fondues. Best of all is the fillet, but roast beef and sirloin tip are also well suited. Ideally beef should be well aged, so ask the butcher. It is also ideal to have the butcher slice it, but only if you will use the meat on the same day; it does not keep as well when sliced. If you prepare the meat yourself, all the sinews and skin must be removed with a sharp knife. According to the recipe, the meat must be cut into paper-thin slices or cubes, as a rule about 3/4 to 1 inch (2 to 3cm). The best way to cut the meat into thin slices is to put it in a freezer bag ahead of time and freeze it about 45 minutes. Cut the partially frozen meat with a sharp knife or slicing machine and arrange quickly on a platter.

   Pork is also good in fondues. Suitable are fillet and cutlets, cut into strips or thin slices (when partially frozen; see above). **Chicken** and **turkey** are excellent in fondues, especially the delicate breast fillets. Poultry is also cut into strips or cubes. As for **duck**, the breast is the usable part. The skin and fatty covering should always be removed. Unusual but very well suited to fondue are **venison** and **rabbit**—just the delicate parts such as the fillet or back loin. All bones and gristle must be carefully removed from game. **Ham** and **sausage** bring variety to the fondue table. Choose lean varieties, as they don't form unhealthy nitrosamines when cooked in hot oil.

Not all the meat, poultry, or fish should be served at one time; reserve a portion on a platter in the refrigerator to be served later in the meal.

If you offer different kinds of meat, arrange it on different platters. The cooking time is determined by the size of the meat pieces and by how well done the meat should be. Pork, poultry, and game must be thoroughly cooked.

Fish and Seafood

With fish and seafood, freshness is most important. Pass on any with a strong fishy smell. Fresh products smell pleasantly of the sea. With finfish, it's easiest to buy fillets; at home you will only need to cut them into bite-size pieces. Freshly caught fish from a fish market is optimum, although frozen fish can also be used for fondue. In any case, fish for fondue should be firm-fleshed so it keeps its shape during cooking. **Salmon**, **red snapper**, **swordfish**, **sole**, **rockfish**, **fresh tuna**, **halibut**, and **haddock** are all excellent, especially for broth fondues. Small fish such as **sardines** can be cooked whole in an oil fondue as they are in Mediterranean cuisine.

   Shrimp—large prawns as well as smaller types—are used cooked or raw, fresh or frozen, and with or without the shells. Raw shrimp should be deveined and, if necessary, the shells can be removed. If you have a choice between raw and cooked shrimp, choose raw—they taste better.

   Some superior fish fondues showcase plenty of **shelled mussels**, available fresh or frozen. **Squid** can be bought frozen in ready-to-serve rings.

Fish fillets must be carefully boned. Stroke the fish carefully with your fingers; when you feel a bone, remove it with tweezers.

Shrimp

Mushrooms

Donggu or black mushrooms are dried Shiitake mushrooms. The stems of Shiitake mushrooms are hard and inedible; therefore please remove them.

Cloud Ear
Mushrooms

Fresh mushrooms are suitable for all broth, oil, and cheese fondues. In each case, large mushrooms should be halved or cut even smaller or they will take too long to cook. With broth fondue, mushrooms are simply speared and cooked gently in the hot broth. In an oil fondue, mushrooms dipped in batter are especially good, but the fungi are also delicious fried au naturel. **Mushrooms** accompanying a cheese fondue are usually sautéed and mixed in to give the cheese their special aroma. Any cultivated mushrooms are suitable; brown **chanterelles** are especially aromatic. **Shiitake** and **oyster mushrooms** are also excellent in fondue.

When shopping, choose mushrooms that are firm and have undamaged caps. They should not be damp or slimy. Store them only briefly in the vegetable bin of the refrigerator, and take them out of any plastic packaging beforehand. **Dried mushrooms** lend a hearty taste to Asian broth fondues, especially the Asian hot pot. **Dried Shiitake**, **cloud ear mushrooms**, and other Asian varieties are available in Asian markets. Cover the dried mushrooms with hot water and let soak for about 30 minutes before using them. After soaking, cut away hard stems.

Vegetables

Firm vegetables such as **eggplant**, **cauliflower**, **broccoli**, **carrots**, **zucchini**, **bell peppers**, **fennel**, and **celery** are excellent in oil fondues. They should be cleaned and divided into bite-size pieces. It is important that the washed vegetables be well dried with a paper towel or a clean kitchen towel so they do not splatter when put into the hot oil.

For broth fondues, at which guests are given a sieve, **cabbage**, **spinach**, and **small beans** can also be used. Blanching is recommended for **cauliflower**, **broccoli**, **green beans**, and **fennel**: The vegetable pieces are dropped into boiling water for 3 minutes, drained, plunged into cold water, drained well, and arranged on platters. With cheese fondue, the vegetables should be precooked for 3 to 5 minutes; only a few types, such as **bell peppers** and **cucumber**, are used raw. Vegetables like **spinach** that are not easy to spear are not suitable for a cheese fondue, since sieves cannot be immersed in the thick cheese mixture.

Plenty of **bamboo shoots** are used with Asian fondues. You can find them in cans or jars in supermarkets and Asian markets.

For garnishes, **green onions** cut into brushes look pretty. Cut the onions into 2-inch (4-cm) pieces. Make several 1/2-inch (1-cm) lengthwise cuts deep in the top and bottom and place the onions in ice water for 30 minutes. The ends will curl out and look like little brushes.

Spicy Accompaniments

The appropriate spices give fondue broths, sauces, and dips distinctive character. Thai **fish sauce**, or *nam pla*, is prepared from fermented fish and gives Asian broths and sauces their piquant aroma.

Anchovies play an important role in Italian fondues. The salted fish fillets, preserved in oil or brine, are found in small jars or cans. Before use, rinse the anchovies under running water and pat dry with paper towels. Anchovies should be used sparingly because of their strong flavor. Leftover anchovies will keep several months in the refrigerator if well covered with liquid.

Soy sauce is indispensable for Far Eastern fondues. The dark variety has a strong flavor and may be quite salty. Light soy sauce is milder in flavor. Japanese soy sauce, or *shoyu*, is made not just from soybeans but also from wheat and barley. Other than these, there is a light, thick, sweet soy sauce from Indonesia. Use them according to the recipe. Like Thai *nam pla*, an assortment of soy sauces is sold in Asian markets and in well-stocked supermarkets.

Rice wine or *sake* is mild and barely sweet; dry sherry can be substituted. **Rice vinegar** is a mild vinegar made from rice wine mash; **cider vinegar** can be substituted if it is thinned with a little water or broth. Various Asian spice pastes are prepared with chili peppers and spell pungency in dips and sauces. **Worcestershire sauce** is a liquid spice concentrate made from lime and tamarind juices, onions, vinegar, and spices. *Nori*, a type of seaweed, is dark green to dark brown and used mainly for sushi rolls. It tastes delicately of the ocean and is rich in minerals such as iodine, iron, and phosphorus.

Not all soy sauce is the same; there are great differences in taste and quality. The best soy sauces develop complex flavor through fermentation of soybeans and a long natural ripening process; check the label for "naturally brewed" or "naturally aged." Cheaper products contain caramel coloring and have less depth of flavor.

Garnishes and Prepared Sauces

Sweet-sour or salty preserves, spicy dips, and sauces are the most frequently used fondue accompaniments. The choice in supermarkets, specialty food stores, and Asian markets is huge. If you want to offer guests a wide selection of garnishes, buy small amounts; otherwise too much is left over in the jars and bottles. Choose garnishes for every taste. Spicy-sweet **chutneys** are well suited to aromatic Asian meat fondues. Sprinkled with julienned fresh mint leaves, a mango or plum chutney not only looks pretty but is vibrant with flavor. Sour preserves are popular with meat fondues. The offerings range from spiced pickles, pearl onions, capers, peppers, peperoncini, and pickled beets to mixed pickles and relishes. Lastly, there are preserved vegetables elegantly flavored with spices. **Vinegared** and **mustard fruits** belong with meat and cheese fondues.

The greatest variety in condiments is among **sauces**. There are mayonnaise-based types like aïoli, garlic mayonnaise, tartar sauce, and remoulade with finely chopped pickles and spices. Mayonnaises can be accented with sun-dried tomatoes, curry, apricots, chilies, or exotic spices. Such sauces are offered with fish and lean meats. More classic accompaniments to meat and fish fondues are cocktail sauces, mustard sauces, and Béarnaise, made with egg yolk, butter, and tarragon—this last is heated just before serving. Cumberland, sauce made with currant jelly, port wine, and spices, is luscious with fondues of duck or game. Horseradish sauces, sometimes mixed with apple, fit well with beef fondues. A wide palette of exotic sauces is offered in ethnic markets: chili sauce in sharp or sweet-sour versions, peanut or saté sauce, sweet-sour ginger and mango sauces, tomato- or fruit-based salsas. These are all good with meat and fish fondues.

Watch for the fat content in mayonnaise products. Traditional mayonnaise contains about 80% fat; reduced-fat versions have less than half that.

Store leftover sauces and preserves tightly sealed in the refrigerator, and use them soon. The solid ingredients should be covered with liquid. Chutneys can be frozen.

Purchased prepared sauces.a

Cheeses

The cheese—mild or sharp, young or aged, soft or hard—determines the character of the fondue. The cheese for a fondue should have a fat content of at least 45%. Buy the cheese unwrapped in a cheese shop or at the deli counter of a well-stocked supermarket—preferably one that does a high-volume business so you can be sure the cheese did not sit too long on the counter. When shopping, watch that the cut surface of the cheese does not look slimy or damp and that it has no dried-out edges.

Some cheese varieties make tried-and-true combinations; for example, a young, mild **Emmentaler** mellows an older, more strongly flavored one. If you can't get a certain type, ask for an appropriate substitute.

Provolone in various shapes

Hard Cheeses

These varieties lend themselves well to grating and also melt well. **Appenzeller**, the aromatic medium-hard cheese from Switzerland, is used mostly as a seasoning in fondue, shredded or cut into small cubes. **Cantal**, a Swiss mountain cheese, tastes hearty and slightly nutty, and is used grated in fondue. **Cheddar**, with its mild, aromatic flavor, is finely diced and may be combined with a full-flavored beer. Finely grated **Emmentaler** and **Gruyère** make up the classic fondue mixture. Gruyère, a hard cheese with a strong, sharp taste, is made in western Switzerland. The best-known fondue cheese, it is more intense than the Emmentaler with which it is traditionally blended.

Slicing Cheeses

Fondue tastes best when made with freshly cubed cheese; it should be grated or diced no more than half a day ahead.

These softer cheeses are finely diced or shredded in fondues. **Bel Paese** is a mild, creamy Italian cheese with a buttery flavor. **Fontina** originates in the Italian valley of Aosta. With its delicate, almost sweet aroma, it is the basis for the classic Italian *Fonduta*. Fontina is not usually mixed with other cheeses, but may be combined with truffles for a really special fondue. **Gouda**, the popular Dutch cheese, ranges from young and mild to aged (over six months) and is strongly flavored.

All Gouda melts well, and a mixture of young and aged ones is delicious. Danish **Havarti** has a strongly piquant taste reminiscent of Tilsit. **Provolone**, available in ball and pear shapes, is a good blending cheese. Young *provolone dolce* has a mild, almost sweet taste, while the longer-aged *provolone piccante* is stronger. **Vacherin** is a classic Swiss fondue cheese that comes in a confusing number of variations. *Vacherin à fondue*, or Freiberger Vacherin, is a piquant type with a fairly soft consistency. It is an important component of the classic Neuenberger cheese fondue, which is made with Gruyère, Emmentaler, and Vacherin. A mixture of Gruyère and Vacherin is also well loved in Switzerland as the so-called *moitié-moitié*, or "half and half." Another type of Vacherin comes from the Jura Mountains in France; this one is a creamy butter cheese that is sold in wooden boxes.

Vacherin

Fresh Cheeses

Too soft to grate, fresh or unripened cheeses are cubed before melting.

Brie, a mild, soft cheese with a white outer rind, originated in France but is now made in a number of countries. For fondue, the rind is removed and the cheese is melted in small cubes. **Feta**, authentically made of sheep's milk, is coarsely grated before melting; it's helpful to place it in the freezer for a short time beforehand. When combined with milder cheeses, **Gorgonzola**, the blue-veined variety from northern Italy, gives fondue an interesting note. **Mascarpone** is a creamy Italian unripened cheese that is almost half fat. It is used mostly for sweet dessert fondues. Though not a typical fondue cheese, **mozzarella** is sometimes mixed in to lend a delicate tangy note. The cow's milk mozzarella typically sold in supermarkets has little distinct taste, but buffalo mozzarella can be superb. **Ricotta** is sometimes found in sweet fondues. **Roquefort**, the wonderful French blue-veined cheese, intensifies the flavor of fondues made with mild cheese varieties. **Goat cheese** gives fondue a unique taste when combined with other cheese types.

Roquefort

Cottage Cheese, Sour Cream, and Crème Fraîche

These mild, creamy, semiliquid cheeses are sometimes found in sweet fondues. **Cottage cheese** may be low fat or creamed; the more fat, the creamier and more delicate the taste. **Sour cream** has a fat content of between 18 and 20%. Light sour cream contains about 40% less fat than regular sour cream. **Crème fraîche**, a richer type of sour cream, has a fat content of at least 30% and is a matured, thickened cream with a slightly tangy, nutty flavor and velvety rich texture, which can vary in thickness from that of commercial sour cream to almost as solid as room-temperature margarine.

Softer cheeses are best cut with a cheese knife, which has perforations in the blade so the cheese does not stick to it.

WITH BROTH

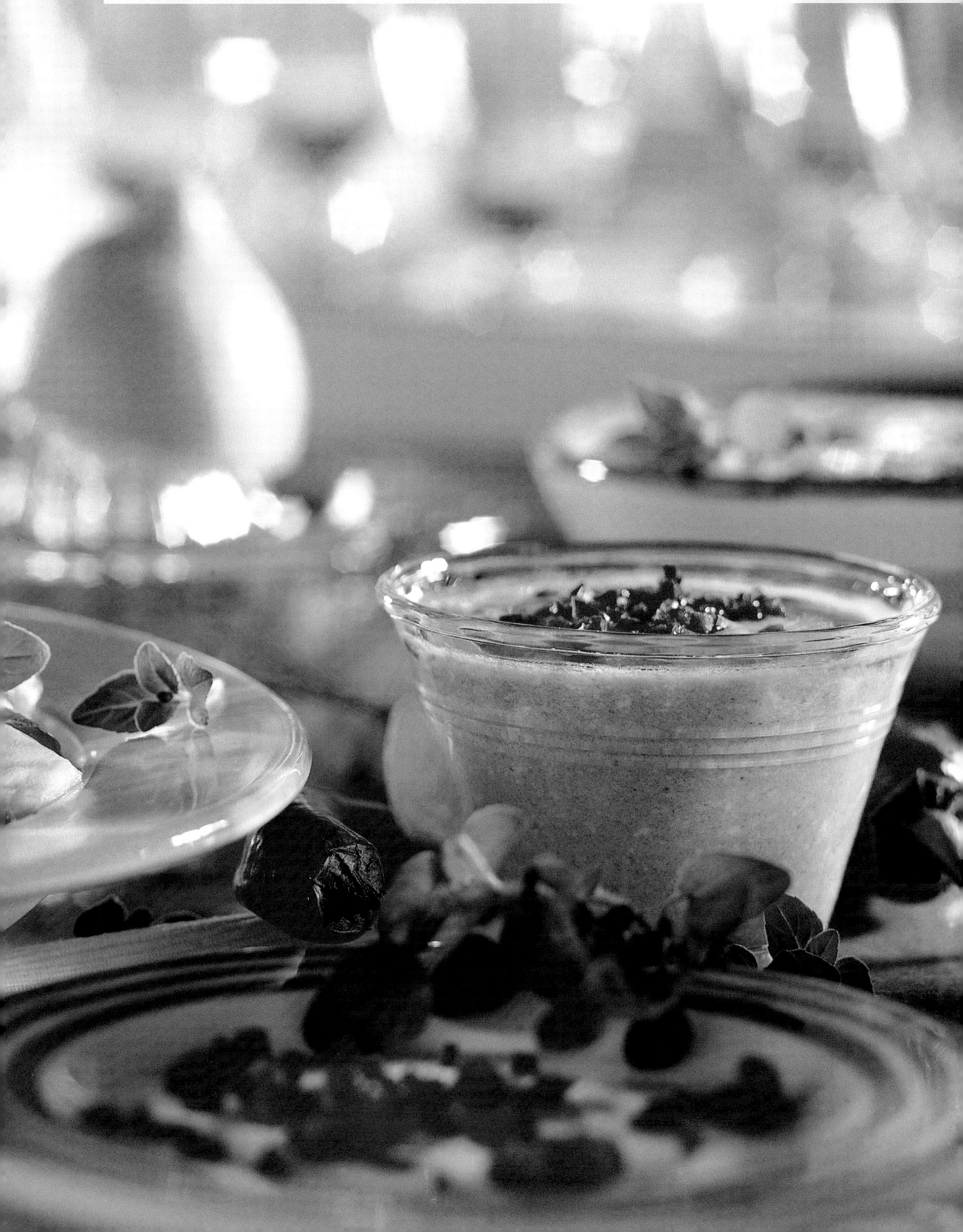

4 servings

Colorful Vegetable Fondue

For the Cheese Sauce:
5 ounces (150 grams) Fontina
2/3 cup (5 ounces/150 ml) milk
5 tablespoons dry white wine
Pepper

For the Tomato Mayonnaise:
2/3 cup (5½ ounces/150 g)
whole-milk plain yogurt
2 tablespoons mayonnaise
3 tablespoons tomato paste
1 tablespoon cognac (optional)
Salt / Pepper

For the Pumpkin Seed Vinaigrette:
1 bunch fresh chervil
3 tablespoons pumpkin seeds
Salt / Pepper
3 tablespoons white wine vinegar
¼ cup (2 ounces/60 ml)
vegetable oil
¼ cup (2 ounces/60 ml) pumpkin
seed oil (available in
specialty shops)

FOR THE FONDUE:
9 ounces (250 g) wide rice noodles
2 red bell peppers
2 yellow squash or zucchini
2 leeks / 2 carrots / 1 small beet
8 ounces (200 g) small mushrooms
3 to 4 quarts (3–4 l) vegetable broth

Vegetarian

1 For the cheese sauce, finely dice the fontina. Bring milk to boil in a saucepan. Melt cheese in it while stirring over medium heat. Let cool.

2 For the tomato mayonnaise, stir yogurt with mayonnaise, tomato paste, and cognac. Season with salt and pepper.

3 For the pumpkin seed vinaigrette, finely chop the chervil and pumpkin seeds. Stir in salt, pepper, vinegar, and oils.

4 For the fondue, place the rice noodles in a bowl, cover with hot water and soak at least 15 minutes. Cut the seeded peppers into small pieces. Thinly slice the zucchini, leeks, and carrots. Cut the beet crosswise into strips. Halve the mushrooms. Drain the noodles and arrange on a platter with the vegetables.

5 Before serving, gently reheat the cheese sauce while blending in wine with a hand mixer. Season with pepper. Pour sauce into small bowls. Bring the broth to boil on the stove. Pour a portion of it into the hot pot or fondue pot and keep at a simmer; keep the remainder hot on the stove for refilling. Cook the vegetables and rice noodles in metal strainers in the hot broth and accompany with the sauces.

Preparation time: 45 min.
Each portion about:
735 calories/ 18 g protein
35 g fat / 77 g carbohydrate

Vegetarian Fondue

4–6 servings
FOR THE FONDUE:
9 ounces (250 g) broccoli
9 ounces (250 g) cauliflower
Salt
9 ounces (250 g) white asparagus
9 ounces (250 g) green asparagus
4 small fennel bulbs
5½ ounces (150 g) small oyster mushrooms
8 ounces (200 g) tofu
3 cups (24 ounces/750 ml) vegetable broth
For the Egg Tomato Sauce:
3 eggs
2 tablespoons tarragon vinegar
5 tablespoons pumpkin seed oil (available at specialty shops)
1 teaspoon honey
White pepper
2 medium tomatoes
2 small pickled gherkins
1 bunch mixed fresh herbs (parsley, dill, tarragon, chervil)
Low calorie

1 Trim broccoli and cauliflower; divide into florets. Blanch in boiling water for 3 minutes. Plunge into cold water and drain.

2 Peel white asparagus, cut off tough ends, and cut the spears into thick diagonal slices. Wash green asparagus, cut off ends and also cut into thick diagonal slices.

3 Trim fennel and halve lengthwise. Cut each half in halves or thirds lengthwise. Trim hard stems from oyster mushrooms. Cut large mushrooms in pieces. Cut tofu into 1- to 1½-inch (2- to 3-cm) pieces. Arrange all these ingredients decoratively on a platter.

4 For the egg sauce, hard-cook eggs for 10 minutes. Cool and chop. Whisk together vinegar, oil, honey, pepper, and salt, and stir into eggs. Halve tomatoes, remove seeds and chop. Finely dice the gherkins. Finely chop herb leaves and mix into sauce with tomatoes and gherkins.

5 Heat the vegetable broth in a pot. Pour part of it into the hot pot or fondue pot and set on the burner. At the table, cook the vegetables, mushrooms, and tofu in the broth and eat with sauce, replenishing broth as needed.

Other good accompaniments:
Remoulade Sauce (p. 59), Mustard Cream (p. 64), Garlic Mayonnaise (p. 43)

*Preparation time: 1¼ hrs.
For 6 persons, each portion about: 295 calories
29 g protein/ 14 g fat /
26 g carbohydrate*

4 servings

FOR THE FONDUE:
11 to 14 ounces (300 to 400 g) skinless, boneless chicken breasts
11 to 14 ounces (300 to 400 g) skinless, boneless turkey breasts
3 tablespoons lemon juice
1 teaspoon Worcestershire sauce
5 ounces (150 g) small mushrooms
4 ounces (100 g) snow peas
½ bunch young carrots
2 kohlrabi
3 to 4 quarts (3 to 4 l) vegetable or chicken broth

For the Curry Cottage Cheese Dip:
2 sour green apples
2 tablespoons lemon juice
2 tablespoons vegetable oil
1 pound (400 g) small-curd cottage cheese
1 tablespoon curry powder
Salt
Pepper

Low calorie

Light Fondue with Poultry and Vegetables

1 Cut poultry into ¾- to 1-inch (2- to 3-cm) cubes. In a bowl, mix with lemon juice and Worcestershire sauce and let marinate.

2 Wipe mushrooms with paper towels or wash quickly. Trim snow peas. Peel carrots and slice diagonally. Peel kohlrabi, halve, and slice. Arrange vegetables and poultry decoratively on a platter.

3 For the curry dip, peel apples and grate finely. Stir with lemon juice, oil, cottage cheese, curry powder, salt, and pepper. Chill until ready to serve.

4 Heat the vegetable or chicken broth in a pot. Pour part of it into the hot pot or fondue pot and set on the burner. At the table, cook the poultry and vegetable pieces in the broth and eat with the dip, replenishing broth as needed.

Other good accompaniments:

Fresh baguette, small pickled gherkins, pearl onions, Chicory Salad (p. 83) or a colorful mixed-leaf salad

Tip: For a pretty garnish, thinly slice lemons, halve the slices, and tuck them into the meat.

Preparation time: 1 hr.
Each portion about:
395 calories / 64 g protein
6 g fat / 25 g carbohydrate

Spring Fondue with Shiitake Mushrooms

4 servings

For the Lemon Sauce:

3 garlic cloves / 2 shallots
2 tablespoons peanut oil
Juice of 4 lemons
1 tablespoon sugar
½ teaspoon sambal oelek
1 bunch chives

FOR THE FONDUE:

11 ounces (300 g) veal cutlets or scaloppini
11 ounces (300 g) sole or flounder fillets
6 ounces (150 g) small carrots
1 tender kohlrabi
1 bunch green onions
6 ounces (150 g) fresh spinach
4 ounces (100 g) fresh shiitake mushrooms
6 ounces (150 g) canned bamboo shoots
2 to 3 quarts (2 to 3 l) chicken broth
3 tablespoons soy sauce
3 tablespoons sake or dry sherry

Low calorie

1 For the sauce, finely chop garlic and shallots. Heat oil in a skillet and sauté garlic and shallots over low heat until translucent. Stir in lemon juice, sugar, and sambal oelek. Bring the sauce to boil, then remove from heat. Chop chives and sprinkle on sauce.

2 Cut meat and fish into thin slices and arrange on a platter. Trim vegetables. Peel carrots and slice thinly. Quarter the kohlrabi and slice thinly. Cut green onions into 2-inch (5-cm) strips. Leave spinach whole. Wipe mushrooms clean, remove stems, and slice caps. Divide bamboo shoots into sticks. Arrange everything decoratively on a platter.

3 Bring 1½ quarts (1.5 l) broth to boil; stir in soy sauce and sake. Pour part of it into the hot pot or fondue pot. At the table, cook foods in the broth with a skewer or fondue strainer, then dunk them in the sauce, replenishing broth as needed.

Other good accompaniments:

Rice or Chinese wheat noodles are tasty with this. Serve the broth at the end.

Tip: You can use dried shiitake instead of fresh mushrooms (you will need 1 ounce/30 g). Soak 30 minutes in hot water, trim off stems and cut the caps into small strips.

> **Preparation time: 45 min.**
> **Each portion about: 320 calories**
> **35 g protein / 10 g fat**
> **23 g carbohydrate**

4 servings

For the Broth:

4 green onions
9 ounces (250 g) carrots
9 ounces (250 g) radishes
2 star anise
½ teaspoon whole black peppercorns
Small piece of fresh ginger
½ cup (4 ounces/125 ml) plum wine / Salt

FOR THE HOT POT:

1 ounce (20 g) dried cloud ear mushrooms
1 pound (500 g) firm tofu
2 small leeks
8 ounces (200 g) baby corn
1 pound (400 g) mushrooms
8 ounces (250 g) leaf spinach
4 ounces (100 g) canned straw mushrooms

For the Spicy Peanut Sauce:

1 teaspoon chili oil
3 tablespoons rice wine
½ cup (4 ounces/125 ml) saté sauce (peanut sauce)
1 tablespoon dark sesame oil
5 tablespoons Chinese soy sauce
1½ teaspoon sugar

Specialty from China

Vegetarian Hot Pot

1 For the broth, wash and finely chop vegetables. Bring 3 quarts (3l) water to boil in a pot. Add vegetables, star anise, and peppercorns and simmer, covered, over low heat for 2 hours. Strain broth. Peel ginger and grate finely. Stir into the broth with plum wine and season with salt.

2 Cover the dried mushrooms with warm water and soak 30 minutes. Cut tofu in cubes. Clean leeks and cut diagonally into 1-inch (2-cm) pieces. Rinse baby corn.

3 Wipe mushrooms with paper towels or wash quickly, then halve or quarter. Wash spinach and cut off tough stems. Drain the soaked mushrooms and straw mushrooms. Arrange the ingredients decoratively on a platter.

4 For the peanut sauce, mix chili oil, rice wine, saté sauce, sesame oil, soy sauce, and sugar. Bring broth to a boil. Pour part of it into a hot pot or fondue pot. At the table, cook ingredients of choice in a strainer and eat with the sauce, replenishing broth as needed. Serve the broth in small bowls at the end.

Tip: Shiitake mushrooms, fresh or dried and soaked, are a good addition to this fondue.

4 servings

1 ounce (20 g) dried porcini
mushrooms
2 green onions
1 walnut-size piece fresh ginger
1 red chili pepper
1¼ quarts (1.25 l) chicken
or beef broth
1¾ quarts (14 ounces/400 ml)
wild mushroom broth (canned,
bouillon cubes)
¼ cup (2 ounces/60 ml)
soy sauce
1½ pounds (600 g) medium
mushrooms
8 beet-green leaves
2 tablespoons butter
2 slices toasted white bread / Salt
White pepper / Cayenne pepper
4 ounces (100 g) ground veal
1 egg yolk
1 tablespoon chopped fresh parsley
3 ounces (80 g) cooked ham
3 ounces (80 g) finely grated
Gouda cheese
1 teaspoon prepared mustard
1 tablespoon crème fraîche or
sour cream

Low calorie

Mushroom Fondue with Beet-Green Rolls

1 Cover the porcini with 2 cups (16 ounces/500 ml) water. Trim green onions; cut one in pieces and chop the other. Peel and slice ginger. Seed the chili.

2 Bring chicken or beef broth to boil. Combine mushroom broth, soy sauce, green onion pieces, ginger, chili and porcini with soaking liquid and simmer over low heat for 30 minutes.

3 Wash mushrooms; carefully twist out stems. Using a melon baller, slightly enlarge the cap openings. Add 6 to 8 of the stems to the mushroom broth. Finely chop the porcini caps and the remaining stems. Blanch beet greens in boiling salted water for 2 minutes. Rinse with cold water and spread out on work surface.

4 Heat butter in a skillet and sauté chopped mushrooms 3 minutes. Chop the toast, pour 4 to 5 tablespoons broth over it and let soak. Mix with sautéed mushrooms and season with salt, pepper, and cayenne. Divide among beet greens. Fold over leaves and roll up.

5 Mix ground veal with egg yolk and parsley. Season with salt and pepper. Using a teaspoon, spread in half the mushroom caps. Finely dice ham and mix with cheese, mustard, and crème fraîche. Season with pepper and cayenne. Press ham mixture into remaining mushroom caps.

6 Strain the mushroom broth into hot pot or fondue pot and set over burner. At the table, cook the filled mushroom caps and beet-green rolls in a fondue strainer in the broth 4 to 5 minutes.

Other good accompaniments:
Lemon Cream (p. 68), lime quarters for sprinkling the mushrooms, fresh baguette, and mixed salad.

Preparation time: 2½ hrs.
Each portion about:
310 calories / 14g protein
18g fat / 27g carbohydrate

Quick Fish Fondue

For the Tomato Sauce:
1 onion / 1 tablespoon olive oil
1 pound (400 g) canned peeled tomatoes
Salt / Pepper
1 tablespoon honey
1 tablespoon balsamic vinegar
1 teaspoon fresh thyme leaves

For the Basil Dip:
2½ ounces (75 g) shallots
2 bunches fresh basil
5 tablespoons balsamic vinegar
Salt / Pepper
½ cup (4 ounces/125 ml) olive oil

FOR THE FONDUE:
4 ounces (100 g) fresh shiitake mushrooms
1 bunch watercress
3 small zucchini
8 ounces (200 g) tuna fillet
8 ounces (200 g) walleye fillet
8 ounces (200 g) salmon fillet
8 ounces (200 g) shelled, deveined shrimp
3¼ cups (26 ounces/800 ml) fish stock
3 quarts (3 l) vegetable broth

Quick to prepare

1 For the tomato sauce, chop the onion. Heat the oil and sauté onion until translucent. Add tomatoes and mash with a fork. Season with salt, pepper, honey, vinegar, and thyme and simmer uncovered over low heat 15 minutes. Season to taste and let cool.

2 For the basil dip, mince shallots. Chop basil leaves. Mix shallots, basil, vinegar, salt, and pepper; beat in oil!.

3 For the fondue, wash the shiitake quickly or wipe with paper towels; cut into smaller pieces if necessary. Remove tough stems from watercress. Trim the zucchini and cut into 1½-inch (4-cm) pieces; quarter these pieces lengthwise. Cut fish fillets into bite-size pieces. Rinse shrimp with cold water and drain well.

4 Arrange all ingredients decoratively on a platter. Divide sauces among small bowls. Heat fish stock and broth until boiling. Pour part of it into hot pot or fondue pot and set over burner. At the table, cook vegetables and fish in the broth and eat with sauces, replenishing broth as needed.

Other good accompaniments:
Two different types bread—for example, white bread and a rustic dark bread—and Garlic Sauce (p. 73).

Preparation time: 45 min.
Each portion about:
505 calories / 42 g protein
27 g fat / 23 g carbohydrate

Wine Fondue with Fish

4 to 6 servings

FOR THE FONDUE:

2 to 2½ pounds (800 to 1000 g) firm fish
fillets (perch, haddock, bass, salmon)
6 jumbo shrimp
6 tablespoons lemon juice
2 to 3 quarts (2 to 3 l) strong fish broth
2 cups (16 ounces/500 ml) dry white
wine or additional fish broth
Lettuce leaves and lemon wedges
for garnish

For the Garlic Mayonnaise:

4 garlic cloves / 2 egg yolks
Salt / White Pepper
¼ teaspoon powdered saffron
1 tablespoon lemon juice
½ cup (4 ounces/125 ml) vegetable oil

For the Coconut Rice:

2 tablespoons oil
9 ounces (250 g) long-grain rice
7 tablespoons unsweetened flaked coconut
1½ ounces (40 g) chopped almonds
2 cups (16 ounces/500 ml) chicken broth

Quick to prepare

1 Pat fish fillets dry and cut into 1-inch (3-cm) cubes. Sprinkle shrimp and fish with lemon juice, cover and refrigerate.

2 For the mayonnaise, force garlic through a garlic press. Whisk egg yolks with garlic, salt, pepper, saffron, and lemon juice until creamy. Whisk in oil little by little until a thick mayonnaise forms. Chill.

3 For the rice, heat oil in a skillet and sauté rice and 5 tablespoons of the coconut until golden. Stir in almonds and pour in chicken broth. Simmer, covered, over low heat 15 minutes. Brown remaining coconut in a dry skillet over low heat; sprinkle over rice.

4 Heat the fish broth, add the wine and pour the mixture into a hot pot or fondue pot. Adjust seasoning. Arrange the fish varieties separately on lettuce leaves on a platter. Garnish with lemon wedges. Cook fish and shrimp in hot broth and eat with the sauce and rice.

Other good accompaniments:
Curry Cottage Cheese Dip (p. 38), Remoulade Sauce (p. 59), Mustard Cream (p. 64), and Tartar Sauce (purchased or use recipe on p. 22).

Preparation time: 50 min.
For 6 persons, each portion about:
720 calories / 46 g protein
41 g fat / 39 g carbohydrate

Elegant Fish Fondue

4 to 6 servings

For the Olive Oil Dip:
4 ounces (100 g) pitted green olives
2 tablespoons lemon juice
1 teaspoon sharp prepared mustard
2 tablespoons balsamic vinegar
Salt
Pepper
1 to 2 teaspoons chopped fresh marjoram
6 tablespoons olive oil

For the Ratatouille Sauce:
1 small onion
1 small red bell pepper
1 small zucchini
1 tablespoon olive oil
½ cup (4 ounces/125 ml) dry red wine or vegetable broth
4 tablespoons tomato paste
1 teaspoon dried Herbes de Provence

For the Saffron Sauce:
5 tablespoons dry white wine, fish stock, or vegetable broth
½ teaspoon powdered saffron
5 ounces (150 g) mascarpone cheese
Salt / White pepper

For the Flounder Rolls:
12 ounces (300 g) flounder fillets
2 tablespoons lemon juice
White pepper
2 tablespoons tomato paste
½ bunch fresh basil
Wooden skewers

For the Fish Balls:
2 slices day-old bread
½ cup (4 ounces/125 ml) lukewarm milk
4 ounces (100 g) smoked fish, such as trout
3 tablespoons minced chives
2 egg yolks
Lemon pepper

For the Shrimp:
1 ounce (30 g) fresh ginger
1 garlic clove
2 tablespoons vegetable oil
8 cooked shelled and deveined jumbo shrimp

Extra:
1 small celery heart
2 carrots
3 to 4 quarts (3 to 4 l) fish or vegetable broth

For skilled cooks

1 For the olive dip, finely chop olives. Mix with lemon juice, mustard, vinegar, salt, pepper, and marjoram, then beat in oil.

2 For the ratatouille sauce, finely chop onion, seeded pepper, and zucchini. Heat oil and sauté vegetables until lightly browned. Pour in wine. Add salt, pepper, tomato paste, and herbs and simmer, covered, over low heat 10 minutes. Uncover and cook until slightly thickened.

3 For the saffron sauce, warm the wine slightly and steep saffron in it until dissolved. Mix with mascarpone and season with salt and pepper.

4 For the flounder rolls, pat fillets dry and cut into strips about 1 inch (3 cm) wide. Season with lemon juice, salt, and pepper. Brush with some tomato paste. Place 2 or 3 basil leaves on each flounder fillet and roll them up. Fasten rolls with wooden skewers.

5 For the fish balls, cut bread into small cubes and mix well with milk in a bowl. Soak for 15 minutes. If necessary, skin the smoked fish. Puree it by pressing it through a fine sieve. Mix with chives, egg yolks, and lemon pepper. Fold in bread cubes. Cover and chill at least 15 minutes, then shape into walnut-size balls.

6 For the shrimp, chop the ginger and garlic. Mix both ginger and garlic with oil, salt, and pepper. Rinse shrimp with cold water, pat dry, and coat with marinade.

7 Trim the celery and cut stalks into diagonal slices. Peel carrots and cut into thin diagonal slices.

8 Arrange all ingredients decoratively on a platter. Divide sauces among small bowls. Heat the broth. Pour part of it into a hot pot or fondue pot and set over the burner. At the table, cook flounder rolls, fish balls, shrimp, and vegetables in a strainer in the broth and eat with the sauces.

Serve a baguette alongside.

Stir the saffron into the warmed wine so that it dissolves.

Push the skewers all the way through the rolls so they hold together well.

Rub the smoked fish through a sieve to eliminate bones.

Preparation time: 2 hrs. For 6 persons, each portion about:
495 calories / 24 g protein
31 g fat / 23 g carbohydrate

Fish Fondue with Creamy Broth

4 to 6 servings

FOR THE FONDUE:
2 pounds (800 g) bones and trimmings from white-fleshed fish
2 parsley roots or 1 bunch parsley
1 onion
1 bay leaf
Salt
6 to 8 ounces (200 to 250 g) *each* fillets of halibut, salmon, haddock, and flounder
Pepper
2 tablespoons lemon juice
2 small carrots
1 leek
2 stalks celery
2 tablespoons butter
½ cup (4 ounces/125 g) crème fraîche or sour cream
1 bunch fresh dill

For the Chili Mayonnaise:
2 egg yolks
1 lime
⅔ cup (5 ounces/150 ml) vegetable oil
6 tablespoons plain yogurt
Pinch of sugar
1 or 2 red chili peppers

For skilled cooks

1 Wash fish bones and trimmings and place in a large pot. Coarsely chop parsley roots and onion and add to pot with bay leaf and 1 teaspoon salt. Pour in 2½ quarts (2.5l) water and bring to boil. Reduce heat and simmer uncovered for 30 minutes.

2 Meanwhile, for the mayonnaise, mix egg yolks with salt and pepper. Pare lime thinly and cut into thin strips; squeeze juice. Add 2 tablespoons juice to the egg yolks. Beat in oil in a thin stream. Fold in yogurt and lime peel. Season with sugar. Seed and mince chilies and fold in.

3 Remove skin and bones from fish and cut into bite-size pieces. Arrange on a platter and season with salt, pepper, and lemon juice. Peel and slice carrots; clean and slice leek and celery.

4 Strain the finished broth through a fine sieve. Heat butter in a hot pot or fondue pot on the stove and sauté vegetables 2 to 3 minutes. Fill with fish broth and bring to boil. Stir in crème fraîche. Finely chop dill leaves. Place half in the creamy broth and sprinkle remainder over the fish.

5 Set fondue pot on the burner and let cream broth simmer gently over low heat. Spear fish pieces on skewers, dip in broth and simmer 3 to 5 minutes. Remove vegetable pieces with fondue strainers. Accompany with dill and chili mayonnaise.

Pour a dry white wine, for example, a dry Riesling.

Preparation time: 1 hr.
For 6 persons, each portion about: / 445 calories
34 g protein / 30 g fat
8 g carbohydrate

Fish Fondue with Beet-Green Rolls

4 servings

FOR THE FONDUE:
2 ounces (50 g) Arborio Rice
Salt
10 large beet-green leaves
8 ounces (200 g) cod fillet
1 tablespoon lemon juice
Pepper / 1 shallot / 1 garlic clove
½ bunch fresh dill
3 ounces (75 g) fresh or
canned crabmeat
1 egg yolk
11 ounces (300 g) baby carrots
3¼ cups (26 ounces/800 ml)
fish broth
2 cups (16 ounces/500 ml) dry white
wine or chicken broth
For the Red Onion Sauce:
8 ounces (200 g) red onions
1 tablespoon olive oil
½ cup (4 ounces/125 ml)
plus 1 tablespoon red wine
or vegetable broth
2 tablespoons red currant or
lingonberry preserves
2 teaspoons balsamic vinegar
1 teaspoon fresh thyme leaves
½ teaspoon cornstarch

Low calorie

1 Cook rice in salted water 20 minutes; drain. Meanwhile, wash beet greens and blanch in boiling salted water 1 minute. Rinse with cold water and drain. Halve leaves lengthwise, cutting out the center ribs.

2 Finely dice fish and marinate in lemon juice, salt, and pepper. Chop shallot and garlic. Finely chop dill. Coarsely puree shallot, garlic, dill, and crabmeat; mix with rice and egg yolk. Season with salt and pepper. Place about 1 teaspoon of mixture on the beet greens and divide fish cubes on top. Roll up leaves to enclose the filling. Peel carrots.

3 For the red onion sauce, finely chop onions. Sauté in oil for 5 minutes or until translucent. Deglaze the pan with ½ cup red wine and stir in preserves. Season with vinegar, thyme, salt, and pepper. Simmer for 10 minutes over low heat. Dissolve cornstarch in the remaining tablespoon of wine and stir into sauce to thicken. Spoon sauce into small bowls.

4 Thinly slice the beet-green stems and carrots. Arrange with the beet-green rolls on a platter.

5 Bring fish broth and wine to boil in a hot pot or fondue pot. Add 2 handfuls of the vegetables and set on the burner. Cook 1 beet-green roll each on a fondue fork in the hot broth for 5 minutes. Cook vegetables and remove with a fondue strainer. Serve with red onion sauce.

Other good accompaniments:
Baguette or rice and Lemon Mayonnaise (p. 95).

Preparation time: 1 hr.
Each portion about:
205 calories / 16 g protein
5 g fat / 20 g carbohydrate

Fish Fondue Canary Island Style

4 servings

1³⁄₄ to 2 pounds (700 to 800 g)
firm fish fillets / 2 onions
¹⁄₄ cup (2 ounces/60 ml) lemon juice
1³⁄₄ cups (14 ounces/400 ml)
fish broth
1 cup (8 ounces/250 ml) dry white
wine or additional fish broth
¹⁄₂ teaspoon whole black
peppercorns
1 dried red chili pepper
4 to 5 saffron threads / Salt

For the Red Mojo Sauce:
4 garlic cloves
2 dried chili peppers
4 teaspoons sweet paprika
¹⁄₂ teaspoon ground cumin
2 slices white bread
¹⁄₂ cup (4 ounces/100 ml) olive oil
4 to 5 tablespoons vinegar

For the Green Mojo Sauce:
4 garlic cloves
1 mild green chili pepper
3 sprigs cilantro
2 teaspoons sweet paprika
¹⁄₂ teaspoon ground cumin
2 slices white bread
¹⁄₂ cup (4 ounces/100 ml) olive oil
4 to 5 tablespoons vinegar

Easy

1 Rinse fish with cold water and cut into 1- to 1¹⁄₄-inch (2- to 3-cm) cubes. Grate 1 onion and mix with lemon juice. Toss fish cubes in onion mixture and chill, covered, 2 to 3 hours.

2 For the broth, mix broth and wine in a large pot, adding enough water to make 2 to 2¹⁄₂ quarts (2 to 2.5 l). Slice remaining onion. Add to broth with peppercorns, chilies, and saffron and simmer over low heat 45 minutes. Season with salt and strain into fondue pot.

3 For the red sauce, chop garlic. Crumble chilies, remove seeds and crush in a mortar with paprika, cumin, garlic, and 1 teaspoon salt. Trim bread crusts. Soak bread in water, squeeze dry, crumble finely, and mix into spice mixture. Beat in olive oil and vinegar.

4 For the green sauce, chop garlic. Seed chili and chop finely. Finely chop herb leaves. Place in mortar with paprika, cumin, and 1 teaspoon salt and mash. Trim bread crusts. Soak bread in water, squeeze dry, crumble, and stir into spice mixture. Beat in oil and vinegar.

5 Set fish cubes with sauces on the table. With broth at the boiling point on the burner, cook fish pieces in the broth in strainers or speared on fondue forks. Eat with the sauces. Serve the broth at the end.

Other good accompaniments:
Small boiled potatoes or baguette and a mixed salad.

Pour a dry white wine.

**Preparation time: 1¹⁄₂ hrs. (+2
to 3 hrs. marinating time)
Each portion about:
555 calories / 43 g protein
32 g fat / 22 g carbohydrate**

Japanese Shrimp Pot

4 servings

FOR THE FONDUE:

1½ to 2 pounds (600 to 800 g) shelled
and deveined large shrimp

½ cup (4 ounces/125 ml) lime or
lemon juice

⅔ cup (5 ounces/150 ml) light soy sauce

6 dried shiitake mushrooms

8 ounces (200 g) tofu

9 ounces (250 g) young spinach leaves

4 ounces (100 g) carrots

4 ounces (100 g) small mushrooms

1 bunch green onions

2 cups (16 ounces/850 ml) fish broth

For the Daikon Dip:

1 pound (400 g) daikon radish

1 teaspoon salt

1 fresh red chili pepper

For the Onion Dip:

2 white onions

2 tablespoons lemon juice

½ teaspoon salt

¼ teaspoon cayenne pepper

Low calorie

1 Rinse and drain shrimp. Sprinkle with 2 tablespoons lime or lemon juice and 1 tablespoon soy sauce. Cover and marinate 1 hour.

2 Soak shiitake in hot water for 30 minutes. Dice tofu. Trim spinach stems and coarsely chop leaves. Peel carrots and cut diagonally into thin slices. Wipe mushrooms with paper towels. Trim green onions and cut diagonally into 1½-inch (4-cm) pieces.

3 Drain shiitake, remove stems, and halve caps. Arrange decoratively on a platter with the vegetables and tofu. Pour remaining lime juice and soy sauce into separate small bowls.

4 For the daikon dip, peel daikon and grate finely. Mix with salt. Seed chili and dice finely. Stir into daikon. Divide dip among small bowls.

5 For the onion dip, peel onions and dice finely. Sprinkle with lemon juice and season with salt and cayenne pepper. Divide among 4 small bowls.

6 Combine fish broth and 1 quart (1 l) water in a hot pot or fondue pot and bring to boil. Add 2 handfuls of vegetables and simmer over low heat for 3 to 4 minutes, then set over burner on the table. Cook food in the broth and remove with fondue strainers. Eat with dips.

As an accompaniment, serve rice or a baguette.

Preparation time: 1 hr. (+1 hr. marinating time) Each portion about: 385 calories / 52 g protein 7 g fat / 27 g carbohydrate

4 to 6 servings

For the Curry Sauce:

1 onion
2 tablespoons vegetable oil
4 tablespoons chopped almonds
3 tablespoons curry powder
1 teaspoon all-purpose flour
$^1/_2$ cup (4 ounces/125 ml) chicken broth
Salt / Pepper

For the Pineapple Dip:

3 green onions
$^1/_4$ cup (2 ounces/60 ml) vegetable oil
16 ounces (400 g) canned pineapple chunks / Few drops Tabasco

FOR THE FONDUE:

1 pound (400 g) firm coconut cream (in one piece)
4 small red chili peppers
2 tablespoons vegetable oil
3 quarts (3 l) chicken broth
1$^1/_4$ pounds (600 g) boneless, skinless chicken breasts
1 pound (400 g) shelled and deveined cooked shrimp
1 bunch watercress or 8 ounces (200 g) spinach leaves
4 firm tomatoes / 1 avocado
$^1/_4$ cup (2 ounces/60 ml) lemon juice

Easy

Caribbean Coconut Fondue

1 For the curry sauce, finely chop onion. Heat oil and sauté onion until translucent. Add almonds and sauté until golden. Stir in curry powder and flour and sauté briefly. Pour in broth. Season with salt and pepper and simmer 5 minutes; let cool.

2 For the pineapple dip, trim green onions and cut diagonally into thin rings. Heat oil and sauté onion rings 2 to 3 minutes. Puree pineapple in food processor or blender. Fold in onions and season with salt, pepper, and Tabasco.

3 For the fondue, grate the coconut cream. Seed and mince chilies. Heat oil in a pot and sauté chilies briefly. Pour in broth. Add coconut cream and let melt while stirring.

4 Cut chicken into thin strips. Trim watercress. Quarter and seed tomatoes; cut into wide strips. Peel, seed, and slice avocado; sprinkle with lemon juice.

5 Pour broth into a pot and bring to boil on the stove. Pour part of it into a hot pot or fondue pot and set on the burner. At the table, cook the chicken, shrimp, and vegetables in the broth and accompany with the sauces. (Just warm the avocado; do not cook or it may become bitter.)

Preparation time: 1$^1/_4$ hrs.
For 6 persons, each
portion about: 270 calories
41 g protein / 45 g fat
32 g carbohydrate

8 ounces (200 g) sushi rice
(a short-grain rice found in
Japanese markets)
¼ cup (2 ounces/60 ml) rice
vinegar
2 thin zucchini
4 ounces (100 g) fresh shiitake
mushrooms
32 shelled crab legs
5 ounces (150 g) swordfish steak
32 tender Chinese cabbage leaves,
all about the same size
32 long chives
1 bunch soup greens
2 to 4 cups (500 ml to 1 l)
fish broth
2 to 4 cups (500 ml to 1 l) vegetable
broth

For the Spicy Sauce:
7 tablespoons light soy sauce
3 tablespoons sake
2 teaspoons pickled ginger
1 tablespoon wasabi (Japanese
green horseradish)

Low calorie

Hot Pot with Sushi Rolls

1 Thoroughly wash rice and drain in a sieve for 30 minutes. Place rice in a pot with 1½ cups (12 ounces/325 ml) water and 1 teaspoon salt, bring to boil and boil 1 minute. Reduce heat to lowest setting, cover, and steam 15 minutes. Mix vinegar into hot rice, using a flat wooden spoon in a chopping motion so rice grains remain whole. Let cool.

2 Trim zucchini and cut into long, thin strips. Remove stems from mushrooms and clean caps carefully. Cut mushroom caps into fine strips. Rinse crab and fish with cold water and pat dry. Cut fish into 32 thin strips. Cut center rib of each cabbage leaf flat.

3 Lay 1 Chinese cabbage leaf on a kitchen towel. Spoon a layer of rice about 1 inch (3 cm) thick on bottom edge. Cover rice with zucchini and mushroom strips, 1 crab leg and 1 strip of fish. Carefully roll up the cabbage leaf, folding in sides. Wrap the roll with a chive and tie in a knot. Repeat with remaining ingredients.

4 Chop soup greens. Combine fish broth and vegetable broth in a hot pot or fondue pot, add soup greens, and simmer 10 minutes.

5 For the sauce, mix soy sauce with sake in a bowl. Chop ginger and add to the sauce with the wasabi. At the table, cook sushi rolls in a simmering broth for 5 to 7 minutes and eat with the spicy sauce.

Tips: At the end, cook soaked transparent noodles in the broth.

Instead of chives, the rolls can be tied with kitchen twine.

Preparation time: 1½ hrs.
Each portion about:
230 calories / 27 g protein
3 g fat / 20 g carbohydrate

Chinese Fondue

6 servings

For the Plum Sauce:
2 garlic cloves
1 piece fresh ginger, about 1 inch (2 cm) long
1 tablespoon peanut oil
½ cup (4 ounces/125 ml) plum sauce
¼ cup (2 ounces/60 ml) soy sauce
3 tablespoons dry sherry
1 tablespoon sugar
1 tablespoon cider vinegar
½ cup (4 ounces/125 ml) chicken broth
2 green onions

For the Soy Sesame Sauce:
2 garlic cloves
2 tablespoons peanut oil
4 tablespoons unshelled sesame seeds
½ cup (4 ounces/125 ml) soy sauce
2 tablespoons Asian sesame oil

For the Sweet and Sour Chili Sauce:
¼ cup (2 ounces/60 ml) purchased sweet-sour chili sauce
2 tablespoons honey
¼ cup (2 ounces/60 ml) cider vinegar
2 tablespoons dry sherry
1 fresh red chili pepper

FOR THE FONDUE:
8 ounces (200 g) beef fillet
8 ounces (200 g) pork fillets or cutlets
8 ounces (200 g) skinless, boneless chicken breasts
8 ounces (200 g) raw shelled and deveined jumbo shrimp
1 ounce (20 g) dried cloud ear mushrooms
5 ounces (150 g) transparent noodles
8 ounces (200 g) long-grain rice
Salt
1 small Chinese cabbage (about 1 pound/400 g)
4 stalks celery
9 ounces (250 g) tender carrots
1 bunch green onions
8 ounces (200 g) canned bamboo shoots
8 ounces (200 g) fresh soybean sprouts
9 ounces (250 g) broccoli florets
3 to 4 quarts (3 to 4 l) chicken broth
2 tablespoons soy sauce

Classic

1 For the plum sauce, finely chop garlic and ginger. Heat oil and sauté garlic and ginger over low heat until aromatic. Stir in plum sauce, soy sauce, sherry, sugar, vinegar, and broth and bring to boil. Simmer over moderate heat 5 minutes or until thickened. Let cool. Trim green onions and cut into very thin rings. Stir into sauce.

2 For the sesame sauce, finely chop garlic and sauté briefly in hot oil over low heat. Add sesame seeds and stir constantly until golden brown. Pour in soy sauce and sesame oil. Remove from heat and let cool.

3 For the sweet and sour sauce, stir chili sauce with the honey, vinegar, and sherry until smooth. Remove seeds from chili and cut chili into very fine dice. Stir into sauce.

4 For the fondue, thinly slice the meats across the grain (see Tip). Rinse shrimp with cold water and pat dry. Arrange meats and shrimp on a platter and chill until ready to serve.

5 Soak cloud ears 30 minutes and transparent noodles 15 minutes in hot water. Cook rice in rapidly boiling salted water for 20 minutes. Drain well and keep warm.

6 Meanwhile, prepare vegetables. Cut Chinese cabbage into ½-inch (1-cm) strips. Thinly slice celery and carrots. Slice green onions and bamboo shoots. Rinse soybean sprouts quickly and drain well. Blanch broccoli florets in boiling salted water 3 minutes; rinse with cold water and drain. Drain soaked mushrooms. Arrange vegetables and mushrooms decoratively on a large platter.

7 Drain transparent noodles and cut smaller with scissors. Place rice and noodles in separate bowls. Divide sauces among small bowls.

8 Pour 1½ quarts (1.5 l) of the broth and the soy sauce into fondue pot and bring to boil. Set pot on the burner. At the table, cook foods in the simmering broth using skewers or fondue strainers; dip into sauces. Accompany with noodles and rice and replenish broth from time to time. At the end, serve the broth with the remaining noodles or rice.

Pour a dry white wine such as dry Riesling.

Info: The traditional Chinese fondue is prepared in a Mongolian hot pot. The center chimney is either filled with charcoal or heated electrically to keep the broth lightly simmering during the entire meal. A fondue pot or wok can of course be substituted.

Tip: To cut meat in very thin slices and thereby shorten the cooking time, place the meat in the freezer for 1 hour and then slice with a very sharp knife.

Simmer the ingredients for the plum sauce before stirring in green onions.

Remove seeds from the chilies before chopping.

Transparent noodles can be very long; they are easier to eat when cut into shorter lengths.

Preparation time: 1½ hrs.
Each portion about:
785 calories / 46 g protein
23 g fat / 98 g carbohydrate

4 servings

Shabu-Shabu

FOR THE FONDUE:
1 pound 6 ounces (600 g)
beef sirloin / 5 green onions
½ small Chinese cabbage
2 whole bamboo shoots (about
10 ounces/280 g) / 3 carrots
8 ounces (200 g) tender
spinach leaves
8 ounces (200 g) mushrooms
2 onions
8 dried shiitake mushrooms
2 ounces (50 g) transparent noodles
8 ounces (200 g) tofu

For the Lemon Soy Sauce:
1 garlic clove
6 tablespoons lemon juice
½ cup (4 ounces/100 ml)
Japanese soy sauce

For the Almond Nori Sauce:
2 tablespoons sesame seeds
2 ounces (50 g) blanched almonds
2 tablespoons Japanese soy sauce
1 tablespoon each sake and rice
vinegar
1 sheet nori (Japanese seaweed)

Additional:
1 daikon radish / 1 chili pepper
3 green onions
3 to 4 quarts (3 to 4 l) chicken broth

Specialty from Japan

1 Place meat in freezer for 2 hours. Shortly before the meal, cut into very thin slices and arrange on a platter. Trim vegetables and mushrooms and cut decoratively. Soak shiitake for 30 minutes and transparent noodles for 15 minutes in hot water, then drain.

2 Cut stems from shiitake and discard. Cut notches in the caps so they look like stars. Cut tofu in bite-size cubes. Arrange everything decoratively on a platter.

3 For the lemon soy sauce, force garlic through a press and mix with lemon juice and soy sauce. For the almond nori sauce, grind 1 tablespoon sesame seeds with almonds in a food processor. Blend in soy sauce, sake, and vinegar. Put the nori in hot water to cover until softened and mix into sauce. Divide both sauces among 4 small bowls. Garnish almond nori sauce with remaining sesame seeds.

4 Peel radish and grate finely. Trim, seed, and mince chili pepper and mix into radish. Trim green onions and slice into fine rings. Divide radish and green onions among separate small bowls.

5 Heat chicken broth and pour part of it into a hot pot or fondue pot. At the table, cook foods in the broth, dip them in a sauce and accompany with radish and green onion rings. At the end, serve the broth.

Accompany the meal with Japanese short-grain rice.

Pour cool beer or sake.

Preparation time: 1¼ hrs.
Each portion about:
640 calories / 52 g protein
24 g fat / 59 g carbohydrate

4 servings

1 pound 6 ounces (600 g) well-marbled beef sirloin
4 ounces (100 g) transparent noodles
2 bunches green onions
½ small Chinese cabbage
2 carrots
2 white onions
8 ounces (200 g) mushrooms or oyster mushrooms
2 cans bamboo shoots
8 ounces (200 g) tofu
½ cup (4 ounces/125 ml) Japanese soy sauce
4 egg yolks
4 ounces (100 g) beef suet
3 tablespoons sugar
½ cup (4 ounces/125 ml) sake
1 cup (8 ounces/250 ml) vegetable broth

Specialty from Japan

Sukiyaki

1 Freeze beef sirloin for 2 hours to firm. Just before preparing sukiyaki, cut beef into very thin slices. Soak transparent noodles 15 minutes in hot water, drain, and cut into thirds. Trim green onions; cut the white and green parts diagonally into bite-size pieces. Trim Chinese cabbage, cut off tough ribs, and cut in pieces. Peel carrots and cut into thin slices. Cut white onions into eighths. Wipe mushrooms or rinse quickly and pat dry, then halve or quarter. Thinly slice bamboo shoots; dice tofu. Arrange all foods decoratively on a platter.

2 Sprinkle 5 or 6 drops soy sauce in each of 4 small bowls. To each add 1 egg yolk and stir. Place a bowl at each setting. Heat a large skillet or wok on the stove and rub with some beef suet. Set on a burner or small electric plate in the middle of the table and keep hot.

3 At the table, brown a portion of the meat slices quickly in the pan and push to one side. Place a small portion of each of the other foods in the pan and also cook quickly. Season everything with some sugar, sake, and the remaining soy sauce. Pour in a little broth and simmer briefly. With the help of a skewer, everyone serves himself from the pan and dunks the hot pieces in the beaten egg yolk. After each portion is eaten, rub the pan again with a little suet.

Tips: The raw egg yolks are optional. Accompany the sukiyaki with hot white rice in small bowls.

Preparation time: 1 hr. (+2 hrs. freezing time) Each portion about: 765 calories / 48 g protein / 36 g fat / 55 g carbohydrate

Spicy Thai Fondue

4 to 6 servings

2 garlic cloves
1 onion
1 ounce (30 g) fresh ginger
1 ounce (20 g) burdock roots
(available at Asian markets)
2 to 3 fresh red chilies
3 stalks lemongrass
2¹/₂ quarts (2.5 l) chicken broth
1 pound (400 g) skinless, boneless
chicken breasts
1 tablespoon cornstarch
8 to 12 raw shelled
and deveined jumbo
shrimp with tails
12 ounces (300 g) flounder
or perch fillet
12 ounces (300 g) fresh spinach
1 long piece lemon rind
3 tablespoons lemon juice
¹/₄ cup (2 ounces/60 ml) fish
sauce *(nam pla)*
¹/₂ bunch cilantro
9 ounces (250 g) rice noodles or
transparent noodles

Easy to prepare

1 For the broth, peel garlic and onion; halve onion. Peel ginger and burdock and cut into thin slices. Seed chilies and cut in rings. Coarsely chop lemongrass. In a pot bring the broth to boil with these chopped vegetables and simmer, covered, over low heat 1 hour.

2 Meanwhile, cut chicken into strips. Dust with cornstarch and press firmly. Rinse shrimp and devein. Cut fish in thin strips. Trim spinach and wash thoroughly.

3 Stir lemon rind and juice into the broth. Let steep 10 minutes. Season broth with the fish sauce and strain into a hot pot or fondue pot. Set on the burner. Place cilantro in the broth. Cook rice noodles in boiling water 4 to 5 minutes, then drain, or let transparent noodles soak in lukewarm water for 15 to 30 minutes.

4 At the table, cook the prepared foods in portions in a fondue strainer. At the end, heat noodles in the broth.

Other good accompaniments:
Coconut Rice (p. 43); fish sauce or soy sauce; finely cut vegetables such as Chinese cabbage, carrots, asparagus, cucumbers, green onions, shiitake mushrooms, or button mushrooms.

Tips from the Pros !

Transparent noodles and rice noodles are traditionally heated in the seasoned broth and eaten as the finale of the meal. Both varieties of noodles must be either quickly cooked or soaked ahead of time. Transparent noodles must be soaked in hot water at least 15 minutes to soften; then they should be cut into shorter lengths with kitchen shears. Rice noodles are thicker and must soak longer or can be cooked a few minutes in boiling water. Drain well and divide among small bowls. If you want to prepare the noodles in advance, cover them with plastic wrap so they do not dry out.

Preparation time: 1¹/₂ hrs.
For 6 persons, each portion
about: 570 calories
32 g protein / 8 g fat
91 g carbohydrate

Mongolian Hot Pot

4 servings

For the Sweet and Sour Tomato Sauce:

16 ounces (400 g) canned peeled tomatoes / 1 tablespoon sugar

2 tablespoons sake

3 tablespoons rice vinegar

5 tablespoons soy sauce / Salt / Pepper

For the Ginger Sauce:

1½ ounces (40 g) fresh ginger

2 garlic cloves / 5 ounces (150 g) cucumber / 2 tablespoons sesame oil

1 tablespoon sambal oelek

2 tablespoons fish sauce *(nam pla)*

FOR THE HOT POT:

4 ounces (100 g) transparent noodles

4 ounces (100 g) Chinese egg noodles

1¾ pounds (800 g) boneless leg of lamb

1 medium Chinese cabbage

5 ounces (150 g) bok choy

8 ounces (200 g) tofu

3 to 4 quarts (3 to 4 l) chicken broth

1 walnut-size piece fresh ginger

Specialty from China

1 For the tomato sauce, press tomatoes with juice through a fine sieve into a pot. Cook, stirring constantly, over medium heat until thickened. Season with sugar, sake, vinegar, soy sauce, salt, and pepper.

2 For the ginger sauce, peel and mince ginger and garlic. Peel cucumbers and grate finely. Gently heat the sesame oil and sauté ginger and garlic briefly. Stir in shredded cucumber and simmer briefly. Stir in sambal oelek and the fish sauce.

3 Pour hot water over transparent noodles and let soak 15 minutes. Cook egg noodles in boiling water according to package directions. Drain. Cut lamb into paper-thin slices.

4 Trim Chinese cabbage and bok choy and cut into 1- to 1¼-inch (2- to 3-cm) strips. Slice tofu. Cut transparent noodles into shorter lengths with scissors. Arrange all foods for serving. Divide sauces among small bowls.

5 Bring chicken broth to boil. Pour enough broth into the hot pot to half fill it; keep remaining broth hot on the stove. Peel ginger and add to hot pot. At the table, cook lamb, vegetables, and tofu in the broth, remove with strainers, and eat with the sauces. At the end, heat noodles in the broth.

Tip: The classic Mongolian Hot Pot is always made with lamb. But you can cook other kinds of meat in the broth too.

Preparation time: 1 hr. Each portion about: 745 calories
61 g protein / 23 g fat
73 g carbohydrate

Korean Hot Pot

4 servings

12 ounces (300 g) beef fillet
2 garlic cloves / 1 teaspoon sugar
10 tablespoons soy sauce
8 tablespoons sake
1 ounce (20 g) dried shiitake
mushrooms
1 tablespoon chopped cilantro
1 teaspoon cornstarch / Pepper
4 ounces (125 g) ground beef round
4 ounces (125 g) raw shelled
and deveined shrimp
9 ounces (250 g) firm fish fillet
2 eggs
1 tablespoon vegetable oil
12 ounces (350 g) mixed carrots,
daikon, cucumber
4 green onions
3½ quarts (3.5 l) beef broth
For the Cilantro Soy Sauce:
2 green onions
2 tablespoons chopped cilantro
5 tablespoons rice vinegar
3 tablespoons sesame oil
½ cup (4 ounces/100 ml) soy sauce
2 teaspoons sugar
For the Nut Sauce:
2 green onions
1 piece fresh ginger
3 tablespoons bottled peanut
(saté) sauce
2 tablespoons sesame oil
½ cup (4 ounces/100 ml) soy sauce

Specialty from Korea

1 Place beef in the freezer for 2 hours. Cut into paper-thin slices and arrange on a plate. Chop garlic. Mix with the sugar and 3 tablespoons each of the soy sauce and sake. Sprinkle meat with the mixture, cover, and chill. Soak mushrooms in hot water 30 minutes.

2 Mix 1 teaspoon of the cilantro with cornstarch, 1 teaspoon each soy sauce and sake, a pinch of pepper and the ground beef. Shape into hazelnut-size balls. Rinse shrimp and fish and pat dry. Cut fish into thin slices.

3 Whisk eggs with 2 teaspoons soy sauce and pepper. In a skillet heat oil over medium heat. Pour in egg mixture and cook until firm. Let cool and cut into pieces.

4 Trim vegetables and cut into thin decorative slices. Cut green onions diagonally in pieces. Drain mushrooms; remove stems. Arrange all foods decoratively on a platter and sprinkle with remaining cilantro.

5 For the cilantro sauce, trim and finely chop green onions. Mix with cilantro, vinegar, sesame oil, soy sauce, and sugar. Thin with water if necessary. For the nut sauce, trim and chop green onions. Peel and grate ginger. Stir both with the peanut sauce, sesame oil, and soy sauce. Thin with water if necessary.

6 Heat broth on the range, seasoning with remaining soy sauce and sake. Pour 2 quarts (2 l) of it into the hot pot, keeping remainder warm. At the table, cook foods in the broth and accompany with sauces.

*Preparation time: 1 hr. (+2 hrs.
freezing time) Each portion
about: 495 calories
41 g protein / 19 g fat
24 g carbohydrate*

Roast Beef Fondue

4 to 6 servings

1³/₄ pounds (800 g) boneless beef loin

¹/₄ cup (2 ounces/60 ml) vegetable oil

2 tablespoons soy sauce

1 tablespoon honey

1 teaspoon grated lemon rind

1 tablespoon dried Herbes de Provence

1 teaspoon cognac (optional)

Salt / Pepper / Cayenne pepper

3 to 4 quarts (3 to 4 l) strong beef broth

For the Kiwi Sauce:

7 kiwis

¹/₄ cup (2 ounces/60 g) powdered sugar

1 tablespoon lemon juice

¹/₂ cup (4 ounces/100 g) heavy cream

For the Remoulade Sauce:

1 medium onion / 2 anchovy fillets

10 capers

2 pickled gherkins with 2 tablespoons juice

1 cup (8 ounces/250 g) mayonnaise

3 tablespoons chopped mixed fresh herbs

1 teaspoon prepared mustard

2 pinches sugar

Easy

1 Cut beef into bite-size cubes. In a bowl, mix oil with soy sauce, honey, lemon peel, dried herbs, cognac, and salt, pepper, and cayenne to taste. Fold in meat cubes and let marinate, covered, 2 to 3 hours.

2 For the kiwi sauce, peel 6 kiwis, puree, and rub through a fine sieve. Mix with powdered sugar and lemon juice. Beat cream until stiff and fold into puree. Season sauce with some salt and 2 pinches cayenne pepper. Chill until ready to serve.

3 For the remoulade sauce, finely chop onion with anchovies, capers, and gherkins. Stir in mayonnaise and season generously with the herbs, mustard, pickle juice, salt, pepper, and sugar.

4 Peel remaining kiwi and cut into wedges. Arrange decoratively on a platter with the beef. Heat beef broth and pour into fondue pot. Set over the burner on the table and place sauces nearby. Spear beef on fondue forks and cook in the hot broth. Eat with the sauces.

Other good accompaniments:

Mint Chutney (p. 68), Cocktail Sauce (p. 68), pearl onions, prepared creamed horseradish, mixed salad, and baguette.

Tips: Instead of baguette offer small boiled potatoes, sautéed in butter until golden brown and sprinkled generously with finely chopped fresh dill.

For an attractive presentation garnish the kiwi sauce with lemon slices and the remoulade sauce with chopped chives.

Preparation time: 1¹/₄ hrs. (+2 to 3 hrs. marinating time) For 6 persons, each portion about: 540 calories / 33 g protein 29 g fat / 40 g carbohydrate

Choice Wine Fondue

4 servings

For the Currant Pear Dip:
1 pear
¹/₄ cup (2 ounces/60 ml) lemon juice
1 tablespoon mayonnaise
¹/₂ cup (4 ounces/100 g) red currant
or lingonberry preserves
Salt / Pepper

For the Yogurt Herb Sauce:
1 bunch mixed fresh herbs
1 garlic clove
2 tablespoons chopped walnuts
²/₃ cup (5 ounces/150 g) plain yogurt
2 tablespoons walnut oil

For the Orange Caramel Dip:
2 oranges / 3 tablespoons sugar
1¹/₂ teaspoon cornstarch
Cayenne pepper

FOR THE FONDUE:
9 ounces (250 g) skinless, boneless
chicken, turkey, or duck breasts
3 tablespoons juniper berries
3 tablespoons chopped fresh
marjoram
¹/₄ cup (2 ounces/60 ml) vegetable
oil / 1 pound (500 g) mushrooms
3 cups (24 ounces/750 ml) dry
white wine
1 quart (1 l) chicken broth

For skilled cooks

1 For the currant pear dip, peel and finely dice pear, removing core. In a small pot, simmer pear with lemon juice over low heat, covered, for 5 minutes. Pour into a bowl and crush with a fork. Mix with mayonnaise, currants, salt, and pepper.

2 For the yogurt herb sauce, wash herbs and dry well; finely chop leaves. Crush garlic and chop walnuts. Mix these ingredients with yogurt and walnut oil, seasoning with salt and pepper.

3 For the orange caramel dip, wash oranges with hot water and dry. Remove rind of 1 orange with a zester. Section 1 orange and dice finely; squeeze juice from the other orange. Melt sugar in a heavy pot over medium heat until caramelized golden brown. Stir in orange juice and rind. Mix cornstarch with 1 tablespoon water until smooth. Pour into orange mixture and bring to boil. Season with salt and cayenne and fold in orange pieces.

4 Cut meat into strips. Crush juniper berries and mix with salt, pepper, marjoram, and oil. Fold in meat. Clean mushrooms; halve if necessary. Arrange all ingredients on the table and divide sauces among small bowls.

5 In a pot, bring wine and broth to boil. Pour half of the mixture into fondue pot and set on the burner; keep remainder hot in the kitchen. At the table, cook meat and mushrooms in the broth and accompany with sauces.

Other good accompaniments:
For a fruity chicory salad, clean chicory and cut into strips. Mix with orange sections and toss with a dressing of sour and sweet creams as well as orange juice.

Preparation time: 1¹/₄ hrs. Each portion about: 690 calories 44 g protein / 38 g fat 44 g carbohydrate

Bollito Misto Fondue

4 to 6 servings

FOR THE FONDUE:

½ teaspoon black peppercorns	
Salt	
1 onion	
2 bay leaves	
1 pound (500 g) beef shoulder or neck	
1 pound 5 ounces (600 g) chicken parts	
11 ounces (300 g) lean veal loin	
1 pickled pork tongue	
2 tender carrots	
4 shallots	
2 stalks celery	
1 leek	
8 ounces (200 g) cooked salami	

For the Pepper Sauce:

2 red bell peppers	
1 small white onion	
2 tablespoons balsamic vinegar	
1 tablespoon dry bread crumbs	
5 tablespoons extra virgin olive oil	
Salt	
1 teaspoon hot paprika	

Takes time

1 Bring 4 quarts (4 l) water to boil with pepper and 1 tablespoon salt. Peel onion and add to pot with bay leaves and meat. Bring to boil, then simmer gently, uncovered, 1 hour. Add chicken and veal and cook 30 to 35 minutes. Simmer tongue separately in unsalted water to cover for 1½ hours.

2 Meanwhile, for the sauce, wash, halve, and clean peppers. Place on a baking sheet rounded side up and broil 8 to 10 minutes, until skin bubbles. Cool a little, then strip off skin.

3 Dice peppers; chop onion. Puree both with vinegar and crumbs. Blend in oil in a thin stream. Season with salt and paprika.

4 Peel carrots and shallots; trim celery and leek. Cut all vegetables diagonally in thin slices. Skin salami and cut into thin slices. Arrange decoratively with the vegetables.

5 Rinse pork tongue with cold water and pull off skin. Skin chicken. Cut all meats into bite-size pieces and arrange on a warmed platter.

6 Bring 1½ quarts (1½ l) broth to boil in the fondue pot and set on burner. Let meat heat again in the broth. At the table, cook vegetables in the broth. Serve with pepper sauce.

Another good accompaniment:
Parsley Caper Sauce (p. 62).

Preparation time: 2 hrs.
For 6 persons, each portion about:
785 calories / 62 g protein
55 g fat / 13 g carbohydrate

4 to 6 servings

1¾ pounds (800 g) boneless leg of lamb

¼ cup (2 ounces/60 ml) extra virgin olive oil

3 tablespoons mild red wine vinegar

8 sprigs fresh thyme

Black pepper

For the Olive Mayonnaise:

2 garlic cloves / 1 egg yolk

1 to 2 tablespoons lemon juice

Salt

⅔ cup (5 ounces/150 ml) vegetable oil

4 ounces (100 g) black olives

For the Parsley Caper Sauce:

3 anchovy fillets

2 bunches parsley

1 tablespoon capers

1 garlic clove

6 tablespoons meat or chicken broth

3 tablespoons dry bread crumbs

⅓ cup (2½ ounces/75 ml) extra virgin olive oil

8 ounces (200 g) small mushrooms

1 tablespoon lemon juice

1 leek

1½ to 2½ quarts (1.5 to 2.5 l) meat broth

For skilled cooks

Lamb Fondue

1 Place meat in freezer for 1 hour, then cut across the grain in paper-thin slices. Brush 2 plates with olive oil and overlap meat slices on them.

2 Whisk vinegar with remaining olive oil. Rinse thyme, strip off leaves and stir in. Sprinkle this marinade over the meat and season generously with pepper. Let marinate, covered, in the refrigerator for 30 minutes.

3 Meanwhile, for the mayonnaise, crush garlic. Beat in egg yolk, lemon juice, salt, and pepper. Beat in the oil in a thin stream. Pit olives, puree in food processor, and fold into the mayonnaise. Place in a small bowl and chill.

4 For the parsley caper sauce, chop anchovy fillets and parsley leaves. Mix with capers and the peeled garlic clove. Puree coarsely in food processor, adding the broth through the feed tube. Beat in the crumbs, oil, salt, and pepper.

5 Wipe mushrooms, and, according to size, halve or quarter. Sprinkle with lemon juice. Clean leek and cut into thin slices. Arrange on a platter.

6 Bring the broth and a few leek rings to boil in fondue pot and set on burner. At the table, spear 1 meat slice and 1 or 2 vegetable pieces on the fondue fork and cook in the gently simmering broth. Dip in the sauces.

Tips: At the end of the meal, season the broth with Madeira or sherry, sprinkle with fresh basil leaves, and offer as soup.

Garnish the olive mayonnaise with fresh basil.

Preparation time: 1¼ hrs.
For 6 persons, each portion
about: 555 calories
22 g protein /49 g fat
9 g carbohydrate

Indian Lamb Fondue

4 to 6 servings

1³/₄ pounds (800 g) boneless
leg of lamb
1-inch (2-cm) piece fresh ginger
2 garlic cloves / Salt
1¹/₂ tablespoons curry powder
2 tablespoons lemon juice

For the Cilantro Chutney:
¹/₂ lemon
1 bunch fresh cilantro (parsley may
be substituted)
1 fresh green chili pepper
1 green onion
4 ounces (100 g) fresh coconut
1 teaspoon black mustard seeds
1 teaspoon ground cumin
2 tablespoons vegetable oil

For the Raita:
¹/₂ cucumber (about 11
ounces/300 g)
1 cup (8 ounces/250 g) plain yogurt
Pepper / Pinch of sugar
1 pound (400 g) cauliflower florets
1 pound 2 ounces (500 g) small
firm tomatoes
1 onion
1 tablespoon clarified butter
1³/₄ quarts (1.75 l) lamb broth
1 tablespoon fresh mint leaves

Takes time

1 Place meat in freezer 1 hour, then cut the meat across the grain in thin slices. Peel ginger and grate finely. Chop garlic. Mix both with 1 teaspoon salt, ¹/₂ tablespoon curry powder and lemon juice. Coat meat with the mixture and chill, covered, 1 hour.

2 For the chutney, peel lemon and chop coarsely. Wash cilantro and coarsely chop leaves. Seed and chop chili. Trim green onion and chop. Puree these ingredients with 1 teaspoon salt, lemon, and 4 to 5 tablespoons water. Coarsely grate coconut and stir in. Sauté mustard seeds and cumin in oil, stirring, for 1 to 2 minutes. Stir into the chutney.

3 For the raita, peel cucumber, shred, and sprinkle with salt. Let stand 20 minutes, then squeeze out excess moisture. Fold into yogurt and season with salt, pepper, and sugar. Cover and chill.

4 Blanch cauliflower in boiling salted water 5 minutes, then rinse with cold water. Core, blanch, peel, and seed tomatoes; cut into quarters.

5 Chop onion. Heat clarified butter in fondue pot and sauté onion until translucent. Dust with remaining curry powder and sauté briefly. Pour in lamb broth and 1¹/₂ quarts (1.5 l) water and bring to boil. Finely chop mint and add.

6 Set broth on the burner. At the table, cook meat and vegetables for 3 to 5 minutes and remove with fondue strainers. Serve the fondue with cilantro chutney and raita as dips.

Pour chilled beer or dry white wine.

Preparation time: 1¹/₄ hrs.
(+1 hr. marinating time) For 6
persons, each portion about:
620 calories / 38 g protein
43 g fat / 21 g carbohydrate

Ham Fondue

4 servings

About 5 ounces (150 g) each cooked
and raw (smoked) ham, thinly sliced
5 ounces (150 g) smoked
turkey breast
5 ounces (150 g) prosciutto,
thinly sliced
1 garlic clove
1 onion
2 tablespoons butter
1 cup (8 ounces/250 ml) dry white
wine or beef broth
1 to 2½ quarts (1 to 2.5 l)
beef broth
1 cup (8 ounces/250 ml)
heavy cream
White pepper
Large pinch of sugar
Freshly grated nutmeg
For the Mustard Cream:
1¼ cup (10 ounces/250 g)
heavy cream
5 tablespoons moderately hot
prepared mustard
1 teaspoon cornstarch
Pepper
½ teaspoon sugar
Salt

Quick to prepare

1 Roll up ham slices, turkey, and prosciutto and arrange separately on a wooden board. Cut rolls into bite-size pieces.

2 Finely chop the garlic and onion. Heat butter in a pot and sauté garlic and onion 2 minutes. Pour in wine and bring to boil. Add broth and cream and season generously with pepper, sugar, and nutmeg. Keep broth hot on the stove, but do not boil.

3 For the mustard cream, whisk cream with mustard and cornstarch in a small saucepan. Bring to boil, stirring constantly, then simmer over low heat 5 minutes. Season with pepper, sugar, and salt.

4 Pour the cream broth into the fondue pot and set on the burner. Serve the mustard sauce hot with the fondue; if possible, keep it warm on a hot plate or burner. Spear ham rolls on fondue forks and heat in the broth. Eat with mustard cream.

Other good accompaniments:

Freshly cooked new potatoes, herb butter, mixed pickles, Remoulade Sauce (p. 59), Potato Lettuce Salad (p. 74), and purchased creamed horseradish.

Tip: If you wish to prepare your own creamed horseradish: Boil 8 ounces (200 g) heavy cream for 7 to 8 minutes or until thick. Peel and grate 8 ounces (200 g) fresh horseradish (or substitute 4 ounces (100 g) drained, bottled horseradish). Stir horseradish and 8 ounces (200 g) cottage cheese into the cream. Season with 1 teaspoon sugar, salt, pepper, and 1 tablespoon vinegar. Cut 1 bunch chives into thin rings and fold in. Serve warm or cold.

Preparation time: 45 min.
Each portion about:
695 calories / 60 g protein
27 g fat / 10 g carbohydrate

Sausage Fondue

4 to 6 servings

12 ounces (350 g) ground beef round

3 small onions

2 tablespoons dry bread crumbs

1 egg / Salt

Black pepper

2 teaspoons sweet paprika

¼ teaspoon hot paprika

12 ounces (350 g) bratwurst

10 ounces (300 g) small cocktail franks, or frankfurters cut into 1½- to 2-inch (4- to 5-cm) pieces

2 cups (16 ounces/500 ml) dry white wine

2 cups (16 ounces/500 ml) vegetable broth

1 bouquet garni (sprigs of fresh parsley, thyme, marjoram, bay leaf)

1 teaspoon whole black peppercorns

For the Horseradish Sauce:

2 tablespoons butter

⅛ cup (1 ounce/20 g) all-purpose flour

½ cup (4 ounces/125 ml) milk

½ cup (4 ounces/125 ml) meat broth

2 to 3 tablespoons grated prepared horseradish

¼ cup (2 ounces/50 g) heavy cream

Economical

1 Place ground beef in a bowl. Peel 1 onion and grate onto beef. Add bread crumbs, egg, salt, pepper, and both types of paprika and knead thoroughly. Shape mixture into sausages about 1 × 2 inches (3 × 6 cm). Arrange on a plate and chill until ready to serve. Twist bratwurst into 2-inch (5-cm) sausages. Drain cocktail franks.

2 For the horseradish sauce, melt butter in a saucepan and mix in flour, stirring. Whisk in milk and broth and cook over medium heat 5 minutes. Season with salt and pepper. Remove from heat and stir in horseradish. Whip the cream to soft peaks and fold in. Season sauce again and keep warm.

3 For the broth, peel and quarter remaining 2 onions and place in a pot with the wine, vegetable broth, and 2 cups (16 ounces/500 ml) water and bring to boil, seasoning lightly with salt. Pour broth into the fondue pot; add the bouquet garni and peppercorns. Keep just under the boiling point. At the table, cook the sausages in the broth. Eat with the sauces.

Other good accompaniments:
Dark bread, baguette, ketchup, and onion rings, slowly sautéed in butter until browned and caramelized.

Preparation time: 45 min.
For 6 persons, each portion
about: 605 calories / 28 g protein
46 g fat / 14 g carbohydrate

WITH OIL

Fondue Bourguignonne

4 to 6 servings	
1¾ pounds (800 to 1000 g) beef fillet	
2 pounds 2 ounces (1 kg) vegetable oil for frying	
For the Cocktail Sauce:	
3 egg yolks	
1 cup (8 ounces/200 ml) vegetable oil	
2 fresh red chili peppers	
1½ tablespoons cognac (optional)	
3 tablespoons ketchup	
1 tablespoon chili sauce	
Salt / Pepper	
For the Mint Chutney:	
3 ounces (80 g) fresh mint leaves	
¼ cup (2 ounces/60 ml) herb vinegar	
2 onions / 2 garlic cloves	
3 fresh green chili peppers	
½ teaspoon ground cumin	
1 teaspoon sugar	
For the Lemon Cream:	
1 lemon	
1 cup (8 ounces/200 g) crème fraîche or sour cream	
1 cup (8 ounces/200 g) plain yogurt	
1 egg yolk	
Pinch of sugar	
Classic	

1 Trim skin and sinews from beef fillet; cut meat into bite-size cubes. Arrange on a platter and chill until serving time.

2 For the cocktail sauce, whisk egg yolks. Whisk in oil in a thin stream until a thick mayonnaise forms. Trim and seed chilies; mince. Reserve a bit of minced chili; stir the remainder into the mayonnaise with cognac, ketchup, and chili sauce. Season with salt and pepper. Spoon sauce into a serving bowl and sprinkle with the reserved chili.

3 For the mint chutney, set aside a few mint leaves for garnish; coarsely chop remaining leaves. Puree with vinegar and ¼ cup (2 ounces/60 ml) water. Finely chop onions and garlic. Trim and seed chili pepper and chop finely. Add to mint with onion and garlic and puree again. Season the chutney with cumin, sugar, and salt to taste. Divide among small bowls and garnish with reserved mint leaves.

4 For the lemon cream, wash lemon and grate or remove rind with a zester. Squeeze 2 tablespoons juice. Mix crème fraîche with yogurt, egg yolk, sugar, lemon rind, and lemon juice. Season generously with salt and pepper.

5 Heat oil in the fondue pot and keep hot on the burner. Arrange meat and sauces on the table. Spear the meat on fondue forks, cook in the hot oil, and eat with the sauces.

Other good accompaniments:
Baguette or baked potatoes, mixed pickles, pearl onions, cornichons, mustard pickles, olives, pickled red beets, Remoulade Sauce (p. 59), horseradish, and leaf lettuce salad.

Preparation time: 2 hrs.
For 6 persons, each portion about: 770 calories / 41 g protein / 60 g fat / 16 g carbohydrate

4 servings

For the Potato Corn Salad:

1 pound 2 ounces (500 g) boiling potatoes

1 pound (400 g) canned corn

1 bunch chives

Pepper / Salt

¼ cup (2 ounces/60 ml) vinegar

6 tablespoons olive oil

2 tablespoons pumpkin seed oil

For the Spicy Almond Sauce:

3 ounces (75 g) almond paste

½ cup (4 ounces/100 ml) chicken broth

2 small chili peppers

A few cilantro leaves

For the Peach Sauce:

1 onion / 2 peaches

1 tablespoon oil

2 tablespoons honey / 1⅓ cup (2½ ounces/75 ml) chicken broth

2 tablespoons wine vinegar

FOR THE FONDUE:

8 ounces (200 g) each beef, pork, and turkey breast fillets

4 small frankfurters

1 red bell pepper / 2 zucchini

9 ounces (250 g) oyster mushrooms

1 quart (1 l) vegetable oil for frying

Easy

Mixed Meat Fondue

1 For the salad, wash potatoes and cook in their jackets. Let cool a little, then peel and slice. Drain corn. Chop chives and stir with pepper, salt, vinegar, and both kinds of oil in a large bowl. Add potato and corn and mix well.

2 For the almond sauce, puree almond paste with the broth. Trim and seed chilies and chop or cut into rings. Chop cilantro. Stir both into almond sauce with salt and pepper.

3 For the peach sauce, finely chop onion. Dip peaches into boiling water, peel, and remove pit. Chop finely. Heat oil in a saucepan and sauté onion until translucent. Add peaches, honey, and broth and simmer 5 minutes over low heat. Season with salt, pepper, and vinegar and let cool.

4 Dice meats and frankfurters into bite-size cubes. Trim pepper and zucchini and cut into pieces. Wipe mushrooms clean.

5 Arrange all ingredients on platters. Divide sauces among small bowls. Heat the oil in fondue pot on the stove, then set on the burner. At the table, spear meat, franks, and vegetables on fondue forks and cook in hot oil. Eat with the potato salad and the sauces.

Other good accompaniments:

Olive Oil Dip (p. 45), Garlic Mayonnaise (p. 43)

Preparation time: 1 hr.
Each portion about:
720 calories / 46 g protein
31 g fat / 70 g carbohydrate

Chopped Meat Fondue

6 servings

For the Meatballs:
2 slices stale bread / 2 onions
6 garlic cloves
1¾ pounds (800 g) mixed
ground meat / 3 eggs
3 tablespoons dry bread crumbs
Salt / Pepper
1 teaspoon chili powder
1 tablespoon each prepared mustard
and tomato paste
4 tablespoons chopped fresh herbs
4 ounces (100 g) sheep cheese
such as feta
4 ounces (100 g) cooked ham
(in one piece)

For the Lamb Rolls:
4 ounces (100 g) pine nuts / 2 eggs
1 pound 2 ounces (500 g)
ground lamb
2 tablespoons dried thyme
Cayenne pepper

For the Yogurt Cinnamon Sauce:
4 garlic cloves
16 ounces (400 g) plain yogurt
1½ teaspoons cinnamon
2 tablespoons vegetable oil
Additional: lettuce leaves, parsley,
cherry tomatoes
1 quart (1 l) vegetable oil for frying

Easy

1 Soak bread in hot water. Finely chop onions and garlic. Squeeze bread well, crumble, and mix with ground meat, onions, garlic, eggs, bread crumbs, salt, pepper, chili powder, mustard, tomato paste, and herbs. Knead to blend well.

2 Cut sheep cheese and ham into ½-inch (1-cm) cubes. One by one, pinch off walnut-size pieces of meat mixture. Press meat flat in palm of hand. Place one cube of sheep cheese per piece on half of the walnut-sized meat pieces, one cube of ham per piece on the other half. Shape meat around the cheese or ham and form meatballs.

3 For the lamb rolls, chop pine nuts and roast until golden brown in a dry skillet over medium heat. Mix with eggs and lamb and season with thyme, cayenne, and salt. Shape into small cylinders.

4 For the yogurt cinnamon sauce, force garlic through a garlic press into a bowl. Stir in yogurt and season with cinnamon, oil, salt, pepper, and cayenne.

5 Arrange meatballs and lamb rolls separately on lettuce leaves. Garnish with parsley and cherry tomatoes. Heat oil in a fondue pot and set on the burner. At the table, cook the meatballs and lamb rolls in the oil, in fondue strainers or speared on forks, for 6 to 7 minutes. Serve with the yogurt sauce.

Tips: The best way to be sure ground meat is fresh is to grind it yourself in a meat grinder or food processor. Buy beef that is not too fatty, and boneless lean lamb shoulder.

The ground meat mixture can also be filled with pitted olives, yellow bell pepper pieces, pearl onions, dried tomatoes, cubes of Gouda, or small mushroom caps.

Preparation time: 1 hr.
Each portion about:
900 calories / 63 g protein
62 g fat / 25 g carbohydrate

Potato Fondue

4 to 6 servings

FOR THE FONDUE:

3 pounds (1.2 kg) small new potatoes
Salt

For the Rosemary Caper Sauce:

2 sprigs fresh rosemary / 2 garlic cloves
½ cup (4 ounces/100 ml) olive oil
3 tablespoons lemon juice
1 tablespoon capers
(+1 tablespoon caper juice)
Pepper

For the Herb Cheese Sauce:

1 bunch mixed fresh herbs
3 green onions
10 ounces (250 g) cottage cheese
⅔ cup (5 ounces/150 g) sour cream
or crème fraîche
2 tablespoons lemon juice
11 ounces (300 g) bacon
11 ounces (300 g) oyster mushrooms
1 bunch fresh sage
Lemon slices for garnish
1 quart (1 l) vegetable oil for frying

Economical

1 Thoroughly wash potatoes and cook, covered with salted water, 15 minutes. Drain. Peel, if necessary, cut into pieces, and place in a bowl.

2 Meanwhile, for the rosemary caper sauce, strip rosemary needles, and coarsely chop garlic. Brown both in a small pan in half the olive oil over medium heat 5 minutes. Strain oil and whisk with lemon juice, caper liquid, and remaining oil. Finely chop capers and mix in. Season the sauce with salt and pepper.

3 For the herb cheese sauce, wash herbs, strip off leaves, and chop finely. Trim green onions and cut into fine rings. Stir cheese and sour cream with lemon juice, salt, and pepper, herbs, and green onion.

4 Cut bacon into strips 1 to 1¼ inches (2 to 3 cm) wide. Wipe mushrooms clean, remove tough stems, and cut coarsely. Strip sage leaves from stems. Arrange bacon, mushrooms, and sage on a platter. Garnish with lemon slices.

5 Heat oil in fondue pot on the stove and set on the burner. At the table, spear pieces of bacon, potato, and mushroom with sage and cook in the hot oil. Eat with rosemary caper sauce and herb cheese sauce.

Other good accompaniments:
Pepper Sauce (p. 61) and prepared butter mixture, for example smoked salmon or lemon butter.

Preparation time: 50 min. For 6 persons, each portion about:
740 calories / 28 g protein
53 g fat / 37 g carbohydrate

Colorful Sausage Fondue

1 For the mustard watercress sauce, melt butter in a saucepan, sprinkle in flour, and stir over medium heat until golden brown. Stir in mustard and broth and simmer 5 minutes. Wash watercress, trim, and fold into sauce. Season with salt and pepper and let cool.

2 For the sweet-hot tomato sauce, simmer vinegar with the tomato paste, sugar, and chilies in a small pot, stirring. Season with salt and pepper. Transfer to a bowl and let cool.

3 For the fondue, cut sausage into bite-size pieces. Wipe mushrooms clean. Halve and clean peppers, then cut into bite-size pieces. Trim and slice zucchini. Arrange all decoratively on platters, dividing sauces among small bowls.

4 Heat oil in fondue pot on the stove, then set on burner. At the table, spear sausage pieces, mushrooms, and vegetable pieces on fondue forks and cook in hot oil. Eat with the sauces.

Other good accompaniments:

Onion or nut bread, various mustards, grated horseradish, pretzels or rolls, pickles, chutney.

Tip: Instead of bread, offer a delicious bread salad: Cut 1 pound (500 g) stale light rye *(Bauernbrot)* into bite-size cubes and sauté until crisp in a little olive oil into which 3 to 4 garlic cloves have been pressed. Cube 12 ounces (300 g) firm tomatoes and slice 1 bunch green onions; mix both with bread. Whisk 5 tablespoons balsamic vinegar with salt, pepper, 1 teaspoon prepared mustard, and 5 tablespoons olive oil until creamy. Toss dressing with the salad.

Preparation time: 45 min.
Each portion about:
765 calories / 19 g protein
61 g fat / 40 g carbohydrate

Batter-Crisped Vegetables

For the Garlic Sauce:
2 slices white bread
¼ cup (2 ounces/50 ml) milk
4 garlic cloves
2 egg yolks
⅓ cup (5 ounces/150 ml) extra virgin olive oil
Salt
Pepper
2 tablespoons lemon juice

For the Batter:
4 medium eggs
¼ cup (2 ounces/60 ml) extra virgin olive oil
¾ cup (4 ounces/100 g) all-purpose flour
½ cup (4 ounces/100 ml) mineral water

FOR THE FONDUE:
1 medium eggplant
2 red bell peppers
2 medium onions
2 medium zucchini
1 bunch parsley
3 to 4 sprigs fresh sage
2 lemons
1 quart (1 l) light vegetable oil for frying

Specialty from Spain

1 For the garlic sauce, trim bread crusts and soak bread in milk. Squeeze dry and crumble finely into a bowl. Force garlic through a garlic press and mix into bread with egg yolks. Whisk in oil drop by drop until a thick sauce forms. Season with salt, pepper, and lemon juice.

2 For the batter, separate eggs. Stir yolks with oil, 1 teaspoon salt, flour, and mineral water until smooth. Let batter rest 20 minutes. Beat egg whites until stiff, fold in, and chill batter.

3 Cut eggplant into slices ¼ inch (5 mm) thick. With a glass, cut out the center (with seeds) of each slice so that only a ring ¼ to ½ inch (.5 to 1 cm) wide remains. Cut peppers in ¼-inch (.5-cm) slices and remove the seeds and membranes. Slice onions into rings. Halve zucchini crosswise. Hollow out with a teaspoon and cut into rings. Arrange vegetables and herbs decoratively on a platter. Quarter lemons and use as garnish.

4 Heat oil in fondue pot on the stove and then set on burner. At the table, spear vegetable rings and herbs on fondue forks, dip in batter, and fry in hot oil until golden brown, 3 to 5 minutes. Sprinkle vegetables with lemon juice and eat with the sauce.

Other good accompaniments:
Sheep cheese such as Manchego, nuts, olives, and small baguette slices.

Pour a dry, fruity Spanish white wine.

Preparation time: 1 hr.
Each portion about:
730 calories / 14 g protein
57 g fat / 40 g carbohydrate

Bavarian Mushroom Fondue

1 Peel and wash potatoes and cut into pieces. Cover with salted water and simmer until tender, about 15 minutes. Wash lettuce and drain well. Drain potatoes, toss briefly over high heat to dry, and press through a ricer. Mix with meat broth until creamy. Season generously with mustard, vinegar, oil, and pepper. Peel onion and apple and grate finely. Wash chives and cut into rings. Stir into dressing with onion and apple.

2 While the potatoes cook, sift flour with cornstarch into a bowl. Separate eggs. Mix yolks, beer, oil, salt, and pepper to taste to form thick batter. Let stand 30 minutes.

3 For the fondue, clean the mushrooms, removing hard stems from the oyster mushrooms. Quickly wash mushrooms and pat dry. Cut the ham into 1-inch (3-cm) strips and the cheese into ¾-inch (2-cm) strips. One by one, place a cheese strip on a ham strip, cover with 1 or 2 sage leaves, roll up lengthwise, and fasten with wooden skewers. Cut lemon into wedges. Arrange mushrooms and ham rolls on lettuce leaves. Garnish with lemon wedges and sage.

4 Heat oil in fondue pot, then set on the burner. Beat egg whites with salt until stiff. Stir beer mixture again and fold in egg whites. Prepare a small bowl of batter for each person. At the table, spear mushrooms and ham rolls on fondue forks, dip into batter and fry in hot oil until golden. Toss lettuce with the dressing and eat alongside.

Other good accompaniments:

Garlic Mayonnaise (p. 43), Remoulade Sauce (p. 59), Tartar Sauce (p. 22), lemon butter, crusty dark bread and, if desired, potato salad. You can also dip small pieces of vegetable, such as zucchini and peppers, into the batter and fry.

Preparation time: 2 hrs.
Each portion about:
610 calories / 29 g protein
20 g fat / 84 g carbohydrate

Bagna Cauda

4 servings

8 ounces (200 g) tender cauliflower
8 ounces (200 g) broccoli florets
8 ounces (200 g) tender carrots
8 ounces (200 g) zucchini
1 small fennel bulb
2 stalks celery
1 red bell pepper
1 yellow bell pepper
8 ounces (200 g) boiling potatoes
4 ounces (100 g) mushrooms
1 to 2 tablespoons lemon juice
Salt
5 tablespoons butter
4 to 6 garlic cloves
1 cup (8 ounces/250 ml) olive oil
10 anchovy fillets

Specialty from Italy

1 Wash vegetables and clean or peel. Separate cauliflower into florets. Leave broccoli florets whole. Cut carrots and zucchini into sticks. Cut fennel into ¼-inch (.5-cm) slices. Cut celery into 1½-inch (4-cm) pieces. Cut peppers into strips. Peel and dice potatoes. Halve mushrooms and sprinkle with lemon juice.

2 Blanch cauliflower, broccoli, fennel, carrots, and celery in boiling salted water 2 minutes. Rinse with cold water and drain. Arrange all decoratively on a platter.

3 In a small pot, melt butter over low heat. Peel garlic and force through a garlic press into it; sauté until golden. Gradually add oil and warm over low heat. Remove from stove.

4 Rinse anchovy fillets. Chop finely and add to sauce. Warm over low heat, stirring, until all ingredients are combined.

5 Place the pan or pot on the burner with a small flame. Arrange prepared ingredients around. Dip vegetables in the hot sauce. Offer white bread or Grissini (thin breadsticks) alongside.

Note: Translated from Italian, this vegetable fondue is called "hot bath." Raw or crisp cooked vegetables are "bathed" according to taste in a hot butter-oil sauce that is strongly flavored with garlic and anchovy. Bagna Cauda originates from the Piedmont and is served mostly as an appetizer.

Tip: It is very tasty when, at the end, you stir some cream or a shot of strong red wine into the sauce. In Piedmont it is traditional to cut 1 white truffle (about 1 ounce/30 g) into paper-thin slices and sprinkle them in the sauce.

Preparation time: 1 hr.
Each portion about:
785 calories / 15 g protein
74 g fat / 21 g carbohydrate

FOR THE FONDUE:

8 thin veal scaloppini (about 3½ ounces/90 g)
Black pepper
8 thin slices prosciutto
8 large sage leaves
1 egg white
1 pound 5 ounces (600 g) boiling potatoes
Salt

For the Pesto:

2 tablespoons pine nuts
2 garlic cloves
1 large bunch fresh basil
2 ounces (50 g) freshly grated Parmesan cheese
½ cup (4 ounces/125 ml) extra virgin olive oil

For the Tomato Arugula Sauce:

1 pound 2 ounces (500 g) tomatoes
2 shallots
1 tablespoon balsamic vinegar
2 to 3 tablespoons extra virgin olive oil
Pepper
1 ounce (30 g) arugula
Sage for garnish
1 quart (1 l) olive oil for frying

Takes time

Italian Fondue

1 Carefully pound the veal until very thin with a meat pounder. Pepper both sides. On each piece of veal place 1 slice of ham and 1 sage leaf. Brush the edges of the veal with beaten egg white and roll meat up tightly. Cover and chill.

2 Cover potatoes with water and boil 15 to 20 minutes until just cooked through. Peel and let cool.

3 For the pesto, toast pine nuts in a dry skillet until golden brown. Peel garlic and chop coarsely. In a mortar, pound basil, pine nuts, garlic, and ½ teaspoon salt into a paste (or use a food processor or blender). Stir in Parmesan. Beat in olive oil in a thin stream.

4 For the tomato arugula sauce, core the tomatoes. Dip into boiling water, peel, seed, and chop. Peel shallots and chop finely. Puree tomatoes, shallots, and vinegar until smooth, adding olive oil. Season with salt and pepper. Remove stems from arugula. Coarsely chop leaves and fold in.

5 Cut veal rolls into ½-inch (1-cm) slices. Quarter potatoes lengthwise. Arrange separately on platters and garnish with sage.

6 Heat olive oil on the stove in fondue pot. Set on burner. At the table, spear a veal roll or a piece of potato and cook in the hot oil one by one. Serve pesto and tomato arugula sauce alongside.

Pour a fresh Italian white wine, such as Galestro.

Preparation time: 1¼ hrs.
For 6 persons, each portion
about: 760 calories
44 g protein / 72 g fat
16 g carbohydrate

4 to 6 servings
For the Almond Cream:
3 ounces (80 g) ground almonds
1¼ cups (10 ounces/250 g)
heavy cream
Salt / Pepper
1 bunch parsley
A few cilantro leaves
For the Orange Salad:
4 oranges
2 red onions
1 tablespoon honey
6 tablespoons olive oil
FOR THE FONDUE:
8 chicken wings
6 tablespoons olive oil
½ teaspoon crushed dried chilies
5 ounces (150 g) pitted prunes
4 ounces (100 g) thinly sliced bacon
8 shelled and deveined
cooked shrimp
2 chorizo sausages (Spanish
hard sausage; do not use
Mexican-style chorizo)
2 bell peppers
2 eggplants
1 quart (1 l) vegetable oil for frying
Easy

Spanish Fondue

1 For the almond cream, toast ground almonds in a small pan over medium heat until golden. Pour in cream and cook, stirring, until sauce is creamy. Season with salt and pepper; let cool. Chop parsley and cilantro and stir into sauce.

2 For the orange salad, peel oranges, removing all white membrane. Cut out orange sections between the membranes, catching all the juice. Thinly slice onions; separate the slices. Mix orange juice with honey and oil and season with salt and pepper. Mix carefully with the oranges and onions.

3 Cleave through chicken wings at the joints. Mix olive oil with the chilies, salt, and pepper. Stir in chicken wings. Cover and chill. Wrap prunes with bacon. Rinse shrimp with cold water and pat dry. Slice chorizo. Halve and seed peppers; cut into strips. Cut eggplant into ¼- to ½-inch (.5- to 1-cm) slices and halve them. Season with salt and pepper.

4 Arrange all ingredients decoratively on platters. Heat oil in fondue pot on the stove, then set on the burner. Spear chicken, bacon-wrapped prunes, sausage, and vegetables on fondue forks and cook in hot oil. Eat with the sauce and the salad.

Serve with a baguette.

Tip: Try this variation for the eggplant: Mix a batter of 2 crushed garlic cloves, 2 eggs, ¼ cup (2 ounces/60 g) all-purpose flour, 5 tablespoons sherry, salt, and pepper. Divide among small bowls and set on the table. Have diners dip the eggplant slices in the batter, then fry in hot oil.

Preparation time: 1 hr.
For 6 persons, each portion
about: 970 calories
33 g protein / 77 g fat
37 g carbohydrate

Mexican Fondue

1 Chop 1 onion and garlic and sauté in butter until translucent. Add drained corn with broth, salt, and pepper. Simmer, covered, over low heat 15 minutes.

2 Finely chop the remaining onion. Peel carrot and grate finely. Add both with the egg to the ground beef and knead in enough bread crumbs to make a firm mixture. Season well with salt, pepper, cayenne, and thyme. Dice cheese. Shape meat mixture into walnut-size balls with a cube of cheese in the middle. Chill meatballs.

3 Puree corn and rub through a sieve. Stir in crème fraîche. Season sauce with cayenne pepper and cumin and cook over high heat 5 to 7 minutes. Transfer sauce to a serving bowl. Mince chives and sprinkle over sauce.

4 Clean leeks and cut into 1-inch (2-cm) slices. Cook ear of corn in salted water 7 minutes, then cook leeks 2 minutes. Rinse with cold water and drain. Cut ear of corn into slices; cut the slices in half. Halve and clean peppers and cut into wide strips. Arrange vegetables and tortilla chips on a platter.

5 Heat oil in fondue pot on the stove, then set on burner on the table. Spear meatballs and vegetable pieces on fondue forks and fry 3 to 4 minutes. Eat with tortilla chips, corn sauce, and taco sauce.

Other good accompaniments:
Avocado Cream (p. 79) and an iceberg lettuce salad.

Preparation time: 1³/₄ hrs.
For 6 persons, each portion
about: 775 calories
33 g protein / 53 g fat
46 g carbohydrate

Tex-Mex Fondue

4 to 6 servings

FOR THE FONDUE:

1 generous pound (400 to 500 g) beef fillet

1 generous pound (400 to 500 g) sliced turkey breast

6 tablespoons balsamic vinegar

½ teaspoon chili powder

2 teaspoons sweet paprika

Lemon slices for garnish

For the Avocado Cream:

2 ripe avocados

3 tablespoons lemon juice

2 tablespoons Worcestershire sauce

1 garlic clove

¼ cup (2 ounces/60 g) crème fraîche or sour cream

Salt / Black pepper

For the Cheese Sauce:

3 tablespoons butter

1 heaping tablespoon all-purpose flour

1¼ cups (10 ounces/350 ml) milk

2 ounces (50 g) freshly grated Emmentaler or Swiss cheese

2 ounces (50 g) freshly grated Parmesan cheese

Pinch of freshly grated nutmeg

1 quart (1 l) vegetable oil for frying

Easy

1 Cut meats into 1-inch (3-cm) cubes. Mix vinegar with chili powder and paprika in a large bowl. Add meats and stir to coat. Marinate, covered, in the refrigerator for at least 1 hour. Arrange on a plate and garnish with lemon slices.

2 For the avocado cream, halve avocados and remove seeds. Scoop pulp out of the skin with a spoon and place in a bowl. Add lemon juice and Worcestershire sauce and puree. Peel garlic and force through a press into the bowl. Fold in crème fraîche, salt, and pepper.

3 For the cheese sauce, heat butter in a pot and sauté flour, stirring. Whisk in milk and bring to boil. Let sauce simmer uncovered over moderate heat 5 minutes, then stir in cheeses and season the sauce with salt, pepper, and nutmeg. Pour into a heatproof bowl and keep warm on a small hot plate.

4 Heat oil in fondue pot. Spear meat pieces on fondue forks and cook in hot oil. Eat with the sauces.

Other good accompaniments:

Taco chips, crusty white bread, and prepared hot sauce.

Preparation time: 1 hr. (+1 hr. marinating time) For 6 persons, each portion about: 560 calories 46 g protein / 34 g fat 9 g carbohydrate

4 servings
For the Tomato Ketchup:
1 pound 2 ounces (500 g) ripe tomatoes
1 onion / 1 garlic clove
1 tablespoon olive oil
2 tablespoons vinegar
1 teaspoon dried Herbes de Provence
Salt / Pepper / 2 teaspoons sugar
For the Herb Remoulade:
⅔ cup (5 ounces/150 g) mayonnaise
1 tablespoon white wine vinegar
2 teaspoons hot prepared mustard
3 anchovy fillets
1 tablespoon capers
3 pickled gherkins
1 handful fresh chervil
2 hard-cooked eggs
FOR THE FONDUE:
10 ounces (300 g) raw turkey breast
10 ounces (300 g) skinless and boneless chicken breast
10 ounces (300 g) cauliflower florets
10 ounces (300 g) broccoli florets
8 ounces (200 g) mushrooms
1 to 2 tablespoons lemon juice
1 ounce (30 g) cornflakes
1 ounce (30 g) sesame seeds
1 quart (1 l) vegetable oil for frying
Easy

Crisp Poultry Fondue

1 For the ketchup, quarter tomatoes. Finely chop onion and garlic; sauté in olive oil 3 minutes. Add tomatoes and season with vinegar, herbs, salt, pepper, and sugar. Simmer uncovered over low heat 30 minutes.

2 Meanwhile, for the remoulade, mix mayonnaise with the vinegar and mustard. Rinse anchovies and chop with capers. Finely dice the gherkins. Tear off chervil leaves and chop finely. Stir anchovies, capers, gherkins, and chervil into the mayonnaise. Shell eggs, chop, and fold in. Place sauce in small bowls.

3 Rub cooked tomatoes through a sieve and cook over high heat 10 minutes until thickened. Let cool.

4 Slice meats. Blanch cauliflower 5 minutes and broccoli 3 minutes in boiling salted water. Rinse with cold water and drain. Wipe mushrooms clean and sprinkle with lemon juice. Arrange poultry and vegetables on a platter. Crush cornflakes and place in a small bowl. Place sesame seeds in another bowl.

5 Heat oil in fondue pot on the stove, then set over a burner. At the table, spear 1 to 2 pieces of meat and 1 piece of vegetable on fondue fork and fry in oil until golden brown on all sides. Roll in cornflake crumbs and sesame seeds and serve with tomato ketchup and herb remoulade. Serve with rustic white bread.

Pour a dry white wine or cold beer.

Preparation time: 1 hr.
Each portion about:
580 calories / 47 g protein
31 g fat / 34 g carbohydrate

4 servings	

For the Lamb Meatballs:

1 pound 2 ounces (500 g) ground lamb
1 large egg yolk
3 tablespoons pine nuts
3 tablespoons dried currants
1 onion / 4 parsley sprigs
½ teaspoon cinnamon
Black pepper / Salt

For the Beef Meatballs:

1 pound 2 ounces (500 g) ground beef
1 large egg yolk
3 tablespoons dry bread crumbs
1 teaspoon sweet paprika
Pinch each of cayenne pepper and ground allspice
½ teaspoon ground cumin
4 tablespoons chopped fresh mint
1 tablespoon chopped cilantro
1 onion

For the Yogurt Herb Dip:

1 pound 2 ounces (500 g) plain yogurt
2 garlic cloves
½ bunch each dill and parsley
1 tablespoon white wine vinegar
1 quart (1 l) olive oil

Easy

Fondue with Spicy Meatballs

1 For the lamb meatballs, combine ground lamb and egg yolk in a bowl. Coarsely chop pine nuts and add to meat with currants. Finely grate in onion. Chop parsley leaves and add with cinnamon, pepper, and salt. Knead all well at least 10 minutes, then shape into walnut-size balls, cover, and chill 1 hour.

2 For the beef meatballs, combine ground beef and egg yolk in a bowl. Add bread crumbs, paprika, cayenne, allspice, cumin, mint, cilantro, and salt. Finely grate in onion. Knead all thoroughly, shape into small balls, and chill.

3 For the dip, place a large coffee filter cone in a sieve, fill with yogurt, and let drain 20 minutes. Place in a bowl. Force garlic through press into the yogurt. Finely chop herb leaves. Add 1 teaspoon salt, vinegar, and 3 tablespoons olive oil to yogurt and mix thoroughly. Chill.

4 Heat remaining olive oil in fondue pot, then set over burner. At the table, fry meatballs on fondue forks or in strainers until golden brown and eat with the dip.

Other good accompaniments:
Flatbread, mixed salad, olives, and pickled small peppers.

Tip: This fondue is also good when made with broth instead of oil.

Pour a red Zinfandel or Merlot.

Preparation time: 1½ hrs.
Each portion about:
815 calories / 63 g protein
52 g fat / 24 g carbohydrate

Wild Game Fondue

6 servings

FOR THE FONDUE:

11 ounces (300 g) saddle of venison
2 tablespoons vegetable oil
8 crushed juniper berries
Black pepper
11 ounces (300 g) rabbit fillet
2 teaspoons dried thyme
3 ounces (80 g) slab bacon, thinly sliced
4 ounces (120 g) pitted prunes
11 ounces (300 g) pork fillet
1 pound 2 ounces (500 g) wild mushrooms
1 onion
1 bunch parsley
3 tablespoons butter

For the Chicory Salad:

1 pound 2 ounces (500 g) chicory
1 lemon
8 ounces (200 g) dates
3 apples
11 ounces (300 g) plain yogurt
2 tablespoons vegetable oil
1/2 teaspoon sugar
Salt
Pepper
2 tablespoons chopped walnuts
Wooden skewers for fastening
1 quart (1 l) vegetable oil for frying
A few lettuce leaves
1 to 2 each pears and fresh figs
1 to 2 tablespoons walnut halves

Takes time

1 Trim all skin and sinews from venison; cut meat into bite-size pieces. In a large bowl, stir oil with juniper berries and pepper and mix with the meat. Cover and marinate.

2 Trim all skin and sinews from rabbit. Thinly slice meat and lightly pound flat. One by one, season with salt and thyme. Lay some bacon and 1 prune on each meat slice (if the prunes are very large, halve them first). Roll up and fasten firmly with small wooden skewers.

3 Carefully cut pork fillet into bite-size cubes. Clean mushrooms, cutting large ones into smaller pieces. Chop onions. Finely chop parsley leaves.

4 For the chicory salad, clean and rinse chicory. Pull off a few outer leaves and set aside. Halve chicory lengthwise, cut out core in a wedge shape and cut head crosswise into strips. Squeeze lemon and sprinkle chicory with the juice. Cut dates open lengthwise and remove pits; cut fruit flesh into thin strips. Peel, quarter, core, and slice apples. Stir yogurt with oil, sugar, some salt, and pepper and toss with chicory, dates, apples, and walnuts. Chill.

5 Heat oil in fondue pot, then set on the burner. Wash lettuce leaves and shake dry. Cut pears and figs in wedges. Remove cores from pears. Arrange meats separately on lettuce leaves and surround decoratively with walnuts and pear and fig wedges.

6 Heat butter in a pan and sauté mushrooms and onion for 10 minutes over medium heat. Season with salt and pepper, sprinkle with parsley, and serve with fondue. At the table, spear meat on fondue forks, cook in hot oil and eat with the mushrooms and the salad.

Other good accompaniments:
Purchased mango chutney, Currant Pear Dip (p. 60), Kiwi Sauce (p. 59), baguette, or potato croquettes.

Tips: You can also use other tender game, such as pheasant breasts or wild duck breast.

Prepare chicory salad with pears instead of apples.

Partial freezing makes the meat easier to cut in thin slices. Roll or pound the slices gently to flatten.

Lay bacon and 1 prune on the seasoned meat slices. Roll up tightly and fasten well with a wooden skewer.

Cut meat in 1-inch (2.5-cm) cubes.

Preparation time: 2 1/2 hrs.
Each portion about:
710 calories / 44 g protein
35 g fat / 60 g carbohydrate

Falafel Fondue

4 to 6 servings

11 to 16 ounces (300 to 400 g)
prepared falafel mix
1 medium onion
1 garlic clove
3 tablespoons each chopped
cilantro and parsley
1 quart (1 l) vegetable oil for frying
For the Sesame Yogurt Sauce:
5 ounces (150 g) tahini (sesame
paste)
6 tablespoons lemon juice
11 ounces (300 g) plain yogurt
1 garlic clove
½ teaspoon ground cumin
Salt
1 fresh green chili pepper
For the Feta Sauce:
5 ounces (150 g) feta cheese
11 ounces (300 g) plain yogurt
Black pepper
1 tablespoon mint

Vegetarian

1 For the falafel, add water to the packaged mix and soak as recommended in package directions. Finely grate onion and garlic. After the soaking time, stir them with the herbs into the falafel dough and shape it into 1½-inch (4-cm) flattened balls. Heat oil at least 1 inch (2.5 cm) deep in a large pan and fry the falafel over medium heat until golden on all sides. Drain on paper towels and set aside.

2 For the sesame yogurt sauce, combine tahini, lemon juice, and yogurt in a mixing bowl. Force garlic through a press. Add cumin and salt and mix well. Clean chili and cut into thin rings. Garnish sauce with them.

3 For the feta sauce, mash cheese finely with a fork and mix with the yogurt. Season with salt and pepper and stir in 2 teaspoons mint. Garnish sauce with remaining mint.

4 Heat oil on the stove, then set on the burner. At the table, fry the falafel until golden brown and eat with the sauces.

Other good accompaniments:
Fresh pita bread and a mixed salad.

A light, dry red wine or *raki*, a Turkish anise liqueur, thinned with ice water, fits well with Falafel Fondue.

Preparation time: 1 hr. (+1 hr. soaking time) For 6 persons, each portion about:
560 calories / 23 g protein
38 g fat / 36 g carbohydrate

4 to 6 servings

FOR THE FONDUE:
1 pound 6 ounces to 1 pound 12 ounces (600 to 800 g) boneless leg of lamb / 1 onion
1 bunch cilantro / Salt / Pepper
½ teaspoon ground cardamom
½ teaspoon ground cumin
Pinch of cinnamon

For the Hummus Dip:
10 ounces (250 g) canned chickpeas
2 ounces (50 g) tahini (sesame seed paste) / 1 garlic clove
2 tablespoons olive oil
¼ cup (2 ounces/50 ml) lemon juice
Sweet paprika

For the Harissa Yogurt Sauce:
5 ounces (150 g) plain yogurt
5 ounces (150 g) sour cream
1 to 2 teaspoons harissa (North African hot sauce) / Ground cumin

Additional:
2 cups (16 ounces/500 ml) vegetable broth
11 ounces (300 g) precooked couscous / 1 red bell pepper
1 yellow bell pepper
5 ounces (150 g) eggplant
1 zucchini
1 quart (1 l) olive oil for frying

Takes time

Moroccan Fondue

1 Trim all fat from meat and cut meat into cubes. Chop onion. Rinse cilantro and coarsely chop leaves. Mix half of it with onion, ½ teaspoon salt, pepper, cardamom, cumin, cinnamon, and meat. Let marinate 1 hour.

2 For the hummus dip, drain chickpeas and coarsely puree. Stir in tahini and 3 tablespoons water to make a soft, smooth paste. Press garlic into it. Mix in olive oil, lemon juice, salt, and pepper, and dust with paprika.

3 For the harissa yogurt sauce, stir yogurt with sour cream. Stir in harissa. Season with salt and cumin.

4 Bring vegetable broth to boil. Pour it over couscous in a bowl and let soak, covered, 20 minutes. Clean peppers, eggplant, and zucchini and cut into pieces. Arrange decoratively on a platter.

5 Heat oil in fondue pot and set on burner. At the table, fry meat and vegetables in hot oil until crisp. Dip in sauces and serve with the couscous.

Tips: This fondue is good with Carrot Orange Salad: Sauté 1 pound 2 ounces (500 g) grated carrots in 2 tablespoons olive oil until crisp-tender. Let cool and mix with the juice of 1 orange, 2 tablespoons walnut oil, 1 tablespoon sugar, ½ teaspoon cinnamon, salt, and pepper.

The fondue is even more attractive when the harissa yogurt sauce is garnished with chili rings and the meat and vegetables are garnished with large parsley leaves.

Preparation time: 1¼ hrs.
For 6 persons, each portion
about: 705 calories
39 g protein / 43 g fat
38 g carbohydrate

4 to 6 servings
For the Meat Skewers:
1¾ pounds (800 g) lamb or pork fillet
2 garlic cloves
1 teaspoon ground cumin
½ teaspoon ground coriander
Pinch of cayenne pepper
2 teaspoons sweet paprika
Pepper
6 tablespoons extra virgin olive oil
1 tablespoon lemon juice
For the Walnut Sauce:
5 ounces (150 g) walnuts
2 slices toast
5 to 6 tablespoons lemon juice
½ cup (4 ounces/100 ml) extra virgin olive oil
2 garlic cloves
Salt
1 package long bamboo skewers
Salt
Lemon slices for garnish
1 quart (1 l) olive oil for frying
Takes time

Fondue with Meat Skewers

1 Cut the meat with the grain into 3-inch (7-cm) thin strips. Crush garlic finely with salt in a mortar and place in a bowl. Add cumin, coriander, cayenne, paprika, pepper, oil, and lemon juice and mix well. Coat meat strips with the marinade and chill, covered, 2 hours.

2 For the sauce, finely grind walnuts (reserving a few for garnish) in a food processor or nut grater and place in a bowl. Trim crusts from bread and soak bread in water. Squeeze dry, crumble finely, and add to walnuts. Stir in lemon juice. Slowly drip in oil, beating to form a paste. Force garlic through a garlic press and mix in. Slowly stir in about ⅔ cup (5 ounces/150 ml) cold water until the sauce becomes creamy. Season sauce with salt and garnish with remaining walnuts.

3 Drain meat strips and spear zigzag fashion on one end of skewers. Arrange on a platter, sprinkle with salt, and garnish with lemon slices. Place sauce on table. Heat oil in fondue pot on the stove, then set on burner. At the table, cook skewers in hot oil until appetizingly brown. Drain and eat with the nut sauce.

Other good accompaniments:
Pita bread or rice and a salad of carrots dressed with olive oil, lemon juice, garlic, and cilantro or parsley.

Pour a fruity, dry white wine.

Preparation time: 1 hr. (+2 hrs. marinating time) For 6 persons, each portion about: 590 calories / 32 g protein 49 g fat / 8 g carbohydrate

Fondue Caribbean Style

4 to 6 servings

1 orange
2 garlic cloves
2 tablespoons soy sauce
2 teaspoons honey
Salt
1/2 teaspoon chopped fresh oregano
Few drops Tabasco
1 pound 2 ounces (520 g) pork fillet
5 ounces (150 g) prunes
3 firm plantains (about 1¾ pounds/750 g)
For the Spicy Prune Sauce:
6 tablespoons prune butter (lekvar)
6 tablespoons tomato ketchup
2 tablespoons lemon juice
2 to 3 drops Angostura bitters
1 to 2 teaspoons sambel oelek
8 ounces (200 g) thinly sliced bacon
Orange slices and fresh oregano for garnish
1 quart (1 l) vegetable oil for frying

Quick to prepare

1 Wash orange in hot water and dry. Finely grate 1 teaspoon rind. Squeeze juice and combine with the rind in a large bowl. Force garlic through a press into it. Mix in soy sauce, honey, salt, oregano, and Tabasco. Cut meat into cubes, mix with the sauce, and chill, covered, 1 hour.

2 Soak prunes in hot water. Peel plantains and simmer in salted water over low heat 10 minutes. Drain and slice.

3 For the sauce, combine prune butter with ketchup and lemon juice in a small saucepan and simmer 5 minutes. Season with Angostura bitters, salt, and sambal oelek. Transfer to a small bowl and let cool.

4 Drain prunes and meat. Halve bacon slices crosswise. Wrap half the meat and prunes with bacon pieces, leaving remaining meat and prunes unwrapped. Arrange on a platter and garnish with oranges and oregano.

5 Heat oil in a fondue pot on the stove, then set on burner. At the table, cook all ingredients in oil. Eat with prune sauce.

Note: Angostura gives the sauce an interesting note. You will find the bitters in liquor stores or the liquor section of a large supermarket.

Preparation time: 30 min. (+1 hr. marinating time) For 6 persons, each portion about: 635 calories 31 g protein / 35 g fat 55 g carbohydrate

Fondue with Saté Skewers

4 to 6 servings

1 pound to 1 pound 2 ounces (400 to 500 g) pork fillet

1 pound to 1 pound 2 ounces (400 to 500 g) skinless, boneless chicken breasts

½ cup (4 ounces/125 ml) sweet Indonesian soy sauce

1 piece fresh ginger (about 1½ inch/4 cm) long

2 garlic cloves

Large pinch of chili powder

Lemongrass for garnish

For the Peanut Sauce:

12 ounces (350 g) crunchy peanut butter

¼ cup (2 ounces/60 ml) sweet Indonesian soy sauce

1 cup (8 ounces/250 ml) milk

3 tablespoons white wine vinegar

1 garlic clove

1 to 2 teaspoons brown sugar

Salt

Pinch of chili powder

Pinch each of dried lemongrass and ground cumin

1 quart (1 l) vegetable oil for frying

Specialty from Indonesia

1 Cut meat into 1-inch (2-cm) cubes. Place soy sauce in a large bowl. Peel ginger and finely grate into it. Force in garlic through a press. Stir in chili powder. Add the meat cubes, toss to coat, and marinate 1 hour, covered, in the refrigerator. Arrange on a platter and garnish with lemongrass.

2 For the peanut sauce, place peanut butter in a saucepan. Stir in soy sauce, milk, and vinegar. Force garlic through a press. Stir in sugar, salt, chili powder, lemongrass, and cumin and heat all slowly until sauce becomes thick and bubbly. Season to taste and pour into a heatproof bowl. Keep sauce warm on a small hot plate.

3 Heat oil in fondue pot on the stove, then set on burner. At the table, each diner takes a few meat pieces on a fondue fork and cooks them in the bubbling oil. Accompany with peanut sauce.

Other good accompaniments:

Steamed Basmati rice, purchased Indonesian mixed pickles, mango chutney, and sweet soy sauce.

Indonesian shrimp chips, called *krupuk*, which can be fried by each diner. Break the chips into pieces about 3 inches (8 cm) across; they will double in size in the hot oil.

Pour cool Pilsner, ginger ale, or a light, dry white wine.

Preparation time: 30 min. (+1 hr. marinating time) For 6 persons, each portion about: 575 calories / 47 g protein 32 g fat / 15 g carbohydrate

4 servings

For the Chili Dip:

4 small red chilies
5 tablespoons vegetable oil
1 tablespoon honey
½ cup (4 ounces/100 ml) soy sauce
½ cup (4 ounces/100 ml) chicken broth

For the Sesame Sauce:

1 tablespoon vegetable oil
1 garlic clove
4 tablespoons sesame seeds
½ cup (4 ounces/100 ml) chicken broth
¼ cup (2 ounces/60 ml) soy sauce
¼ cup (2 ounces/60 ml) sake
Pepper

FOR THE FONDUE:

8 ounces (200 g) raw shelled and deveined shrimp
1 pound (400 g) broccoli
12 ounces (300 g) zucchini
12 ounces (300 g) thin green beans
Salt / Flour for breading
1 quart (1 l) vegetable oil for frying
2 egg yolks
1 cup (4 ounces/125 g) all-purpose flour

Specialty from Japan

Tempura

1 For the chili dip, seed and finely chop chilies. Stir with the oil, honey, soy sauce, and broth.

2 For the sesame sauce, slightly heat oil in a pan. Force garlic through a press into it, then add sesame seeds and brown for a short time. Pour in broth. Remove from heat and stir in soy sauce, sake, and pepper to taste.

3 Rinse shrimp, drain well, and dry. Cut the broccoli into small florets. Slice zucchini, halving very large slices. Leave beans whole.

4 Bring plenty of salted water to boil in a large pot. One after the other, precook the vegetables until crisp-tender: broccoli 4 minutes, zucchini 2 minutes, beans 5 minutes. Lift cooked vegetables out of the water with a slotted spoon, drain, and rinse with cold water. Drain well.

5 Dust prepared vegetables and shrimp with flour, shaking off excess. Arrange all on platters.

6 Heat oil for frying in fondue pot, then set on burner. Shortly before serving, mix the egg yolks, 1 cup (8 ounces/250 ml) ice water, the flour and ½ teaspoon salt. Divide the batter among individual small bowls. At the table, dip food in the batter and cook in hot oil. Drain quickly and eat with the sauces.

Other good accompaniments:
Soy sauce and wasabi (Japanese green horseradish) or other grated horseradish. Or a daikon (white radish) salad: Peel 1 large daikon and shred coarsely. Sprinkle with salt and let stand 10 minutes to drain, then squeeze out excess moisture. Trim 1 bunch green onions and slice finely on the diagonal. Mix with daikon. Peel 1 ounce (30 g) fresh ginger and 2 garlic cloves and chop. Mix with 2 tablespoons rice vinegar, 2 tablespoons sake, ¼ cup (2 ounces/60 ml) light soy sauce, and ¼ cup (2 ounces/60 ml) vegetable oil. Toss with the vegetables.

Preparation time: 1 hr.
Each portion about:
650 calories / 24 g protein
46 g fat / 31 g carbohydrate

2 duck breast fillets, about 12
ounces (350 g) each
1 cup (8 ounces/225 ml)
sake or sherry
14 tablespoons soy sauce
2 teaspoons sesame oil
2 teaspoons cornstarch
1 piece fresh ginger (about
1½ inch/4 cm long)
2 garlic cloves
1 to 2 fresh chili peppers
3 tablespoons vegetable oil
¼ cup (2 ounces/60 ml)
cider vinegar
2 tablespoons sugar
2 cups (16 ounces/400 g)
tomato puree
Salt
Pepper
1 bunch green onions
1 red bell pepper
1 green bell pepper
6 ounces (125 g) fresh shiitake or
small portobello mushrooms
1 quart (1 l) vegetable oil for frying

For skilled cooks

Fondue with Duck Breast

1 Cut duck breast fillets diagonally with the grain into paper-thin slices.

2 In a bowl, mix ½ cup (4 ounces/100 ml) sake with 3½ tablespoons soy sauce, the sesame oil, and the cornstarch. Peel ginger and grate half of it into the sake mixture. Coat the meat with marinade and chill, covered, 30 minutes.

3 For the chili sauce, peel 1 garlic clove and chop finely with remaining ginger. Seed and mince chilies. Heat 1 tablespoon oil and sauté garlic, ginger, and chilies briefly over low heat. Stir in the vinegar, 3½ tablespoons soy sauce, 1 tablespoon sugar, and tomatoes. Cover and simmer over low heat 20 minutes. Season with salt and pepper and let cool.

4 For the sake dip, force the remaining garlic through a garlic press. Stir in 1 tablespoon sugar, the remaining 7 tablespoons soy sauce, ½ cup (4 ounces/125 ml) sake and the remaining oil. Trim and finely chop green onion and stir in.

5 Halve and clean peppers and cut into pieces. Wipe the mushrooms and remove stems. Halve or quarter mushroom caps. Trim the remaining green onions and cut into strips. Arrange vegetables on a platter.

6 Heat oil until very hot in fondue pot and set on burner. At the table, fry 1 to 2 meat slices at a time, with or without vegetables, until crisp. Serve with chili sauce and sake dip.

Tip: Place duck breast in the freezer for 1 hour to make it easier to slice.

Preparation time: 1 hr.
Each portion about:
665 calories / 37 g protein
43 g fat / 26 g carbohydrate

Vietnamese Meatball Fondue

4 servings

FOR THE FONDUE:

1 garlic clove	
1 piece (1 inch/2 cm) fresh ginger	
2 green onions	
1 pound 2 ounces (500 g) lean mixed ground meat	
1 tablespoon vegetable oil	
Salt / Pepper	

For the Peanut Dip:

1 garlic clove	
4 ounces (100 g) crunchy peanut butter	
1 teaspoon sambal oelek	
2 tablespoons lemon juice	
2 tablespoons soy sauce	
1 cup (8 ounces/250 ml) canned coconut milk	

For the Lemon Fish Sauce:

2 tablespoons lemon juice	
2 teaspoons sugar	
6 tablespoons fish sauce *(nam pla)*	
2 ounces (50 g) carrots	

Additional:

8 ounces (200 g) iceberg lettuce	
5 ounces (150 g) soybean sprouts	
5 ounces (150 g) carrots	
8 ounces (200 g) daikon (white radish)	
8 ounces (200 g) cucumber	
½ bunch cilantro or parsley	
1 quart (1 l) vegetable oil for frying	

Quick to prepare

1 Peel garlic and ginger; trim green onions. Chop these ingredients finely and mix well with ground meat, oil, salt, and pepper. With damp hands, shape into walnut-size balls and chill on a plate.

2 For the peanut dip, force garlic through a press. Puree with the peanut butter, sambal oelek, lemon juice, and soy sauce until smooth. Stir in coconut milk, salt, and pepper.

3 For the lemon fish sauce, mix lemon juice with sugar, fish sauce, and 6 tablespoons water. Peel carrots and coarsely grate into sauce. Divide sauce among 4 small bowls.

4 Wash lettuce and sprouts. Pull lettuce apart. Peel carrots, daikon, and cucumber and cut into thin sticks. Tear off cilantro leaves.

5 Heat oil until very hot in fondue pot; set on burner. At the table, fry meatballs in hot oil 2 to 3 minutes. Offer peanut dip and lemon fish sauce with the meatballs and as a dressing for the raw foods.

Preparation time: 45 min.
Each portion about:
800 calories / 36 g protein
65 g fat / 18 g carbohydrate

4 servings
16 frozen spring roll wrappers
2 stalks lemongrass
4 green onions
2 garlic cloves
8 ounces (200 g) mushrooms
8 ounces (200 g) Chinese cabbage
8 ounces (200 g) skinless, boneless chicken breasts
3 tablespoons sesame oil
¼ cup (2 ounces/60 ml) soy sauce
Salt
Pinch of cayenne pepper
1 egg white
1 quart (1 l) vegetable oil for frying
For the Ajvar Sauce:
3 shallots / 1 garlic clove
2 tablespoons vegetable oil
¼ teaspoon each ground ginger, powdered lemongrass, and powdered burdock (available at Asian markets)
2 tablespoons soy sauce
2 teaspoons balsamic vinegar
⅔ cup (5 ounces/150 g) ajvar (sweet red pepper paste from a jar)
For skilled cooks

Fondue with Spring Rolls

1 Thaw spring roll wrappers. Cut the bright parts of lemongrass into very fine rings. Trim and chop green onions. Chop garlic. Clean mushrooms and cut into small pieces. Cut Chinese cabbage into very fine strips. Dice chicken.

2 Heat sesame oil in a large skillet and sauté the green onions, then the lemongrass and garlic. Add chicken, mushrooms, and Chinese cabbage and sauté, stirring, 5 minutes over medium heat. Season with soy sauce, salt, and cayenne and let cool.

3 Spread the spring roll wrappers on a work surface and cut in half. Put 1 tablespoon filling on each half. Turn in the dough edges and roll up; do not roll the spring rolls too tightly. Brush the seam with egg white and press firmly.

4 For the ajvar sauce, chop the shallots and garlic. Heat oil in a skillet and sauté ginger, lemongrass, and burdock powder briefly, then the shallots and garlic. Stir in soy sauce, vinegar, ajvar, and ¼ cup (2 ounces/60 ml) water and bring to boil. Remove from heat and let cool.

5 Heat oil in fondue pot. At the table, fry the spring rolls a few at a time until golden. Eat with the sauce.

Other good accompaniments:
Various soy sauces, steamed Basmati rice, Asian mixed pickles, and spicy mango chutney.

Preparation time: 1¼ hrs.
Each portion about:
425 calories / 15 g protein
36 g fat / 12 g carbohydrate

4 to 6 servings

1 pound (450 g) tempeh
1 pound (450 g) firm smoked tofu
2 garlic cloves
6 tablespoons soy sauce
1 teaspoon powdered lemongrass
Large pinch of chili powder
1 quart (1 l) vegetable
oil for frying

For the Cilantro Sauce:
1 large bunch cilantro
2 garlic cloves
¼ cup (2 ounces/60 ml)
rice vinegar
5 tablespoons sesame oil
¼ cup (2 ounces/50 ml)
vegetable broth
Salt
1 fresh red chili

For the Mango Sauce:
½ cup (4 ounces/100 g)
sweet-hot mango chutney
½ cup (4 ounces/100 g) low-fat
cottage cheese
½ cup (4 ounces/100 g) plain yogurt
1 to 2 tablespoons lemon juice
Lime leaves for garnish

Vegetarian

Tofu and Tempeh Fondue

1 Cut tempeh into 1½-inch (4-cm) cubes and tofu into 1-inch (3-cm) cubes. Force garlic through a press into a bowl. Stir in soy sauce, lemongrass, and chili powder. Carefully fold in tempeh and tofu. Cover and marinate in refrigerator 1 hour, stirring gently a few times.

2 For the cilantro sauce, wash cilantro and shake dry. Finely chop leaves and place in a bowl. Force in garlic through a press. Stir in vinegar, sesame oil, and vegetable broth and season well with salt. Clean chilies and cut into thin rings. Garnish sauce with them and chill until ready to serve.

3 For the mango sauce, blend chutney, cottage cheese, and yogurt with a hand blender. Season with salt and lemon juice. Place in serving bowl, cover, and chill until ready to serve. Garnish with lime leaves.

4 Heat oil in fondue pot. At the table, spear tempeh and tofu cubes on fondue forks and fry until golden brown. Serve with the prepared sauces.

Other good accompaniments:
Steamed Basmati rice and Peanut Sauce (p. 88).

Tip: Tempeh and smoked tofu are available in natural food stores.

Pour a chilled Asian beer or jasmine tea.

Preparation time: 50 min. (+1 hr. marinating time) For 6 persons, each portion about: 600 calories / 31 g protein 41 g fat / 34 g carbohydrate

Fish Fondue

4 to 6 servings

FOR THE FONDUE:
8 ounces (200 g) cod fillet
8 ounces (200 g) tuna fillet
8 ounces (200 g) salmon fillet
8 ounces (200 g) swordfish fillet
6 ounces (150 g) small squid
5 tablespoons lemon juice
Salt / Pepper
1 pound (400 g) hearts of palm
8 ounces (200 g) cherry tomatoes
½ cup (4 ounces/100 g) mayonnaise
A few basil leaves

For the Spicy Lime Sauce:
5 ounces (150 g) green onions
3 garlic cloves
3 red chilies
3 tablespoons vegetable oil
2 limes or lemons
1 teaspoon brown sugar

For the Avocado Chervil Dip:
½ lemon
1 large ripe avocado
1 garlic clove
½ cup (4 ounces/100 g) heavy cream
Handful of fresh chervil
1 quart (1 l) vegetable oil for frying

Easy

1 Wash fish and squid and cut into bite-size pieces. Arrange on a platter and sprinkle with 3 tablespoons lemon juice, salt, and pepper. Marinate, covered, 30 minutes.

2 Meanwhile, drain and slice hearts of palm. Halve the tomatoes. Mix mayonnaise with remaining lemon juice, salt, and pepper. Carefully fold in hearts of palm and tomatoes. Garnish with basil leaves.

3 For the spicy lime sauce, trim green onions and chop finely. Finely chop garlic. Seed and finely dice chilies. Heat oil and sauté green onions, garlic, and chilies over low heat 5 minutes. Finely grate the lime rind. Squeeze both limes and mix with rind into sautéed vegetables. Season sauce with sugar and salt.

4 For the avocado chervil dip, finely grate rind from lemon half; squeeze juice. Halve avocado, remove seed, and scoop out flesh. Sprinkle immediately with lemon juice. Force in garlic through garlic press and puree until smooth, slowly blending in cream. Season with salt and pepper. Finely chop chervil leaves and fold into avocado cream.

5 Heat oil in fondue pot on the stove, then set on burner. At the table, spear 1 or 2 fish pieces on a fondue fork (or use a fondue strainer) and fry in hot oil. Eat with the avocado dip, the lime sauce, and the hearts of palm cocktail.

A dry California or French white wine will round out the fondue.

Preparation time: 1¼ hrs.
For 6 persons, each portion
about: 675 calories
33 g protein / 50 g fat
31 g carbohydrate

Fish Stick Fondue

4 servings

For the Lemon Mayonnaise:
⅔ cup (5 ounces/150 g) mayonnaise
½ cup (4 ounces/100 g) plain yogurt
1 teaspoon prepared mustard
1 lemon / Salt / Pepper

For the Tomato Dip:
2 cups (16 ounces/400 g) canned diced tomatoes
1 tablespoon red wine vinegar
1 to 2 cloves garlic
3 tablespoons extra virgin olive oil
1 bunch fresh basil

FOR THE FONDUE:
1 pound 6 ounces (600 g) frozen fish sticks
1 each red, yellow, and green bell pepper
1 lemon
1 quart (1 l) vegetable oil for frying

Quick to prepare

1 For the lemon mayonnaise, stir mayonnaise with the yogurt and mustard. Wash the lemon with hot water and finely grate about 1 teaspoon rind. Cut off some of the rind and cut into thin strips. Squeeze 2 tablespoons lemon juice and mix into the mayonnaise with grated rind. Season with salt and pepper. Divide among 4 small bowls and garnish with strips of rind.

2 For the tomato dip, season the tomatoes with the vinegar, salt, and pepper. Press in garlic and stir in olive oil. Set aside a few basil leaves for garnish; finely chop remainder and mix in. Divide sauce among 4 small bowls and garnish with basil leaves.

3 Cut the frozen fish sticks crosswise into 3 pieces. Halve and clean peppers and cut into pieces. Cut lemon into wedges. Arrange all ingredients decoratively.

4 Heat oil in fondue pot on the stove, then set on the burner. At the table, fry fish and peppers until golden brown. Sprinkle with lemon and pass the sauces.

Other good accompaniments:
Potato salad with a vinaigrette dressing or a green salad.

Tip: Breaded frozen fish fillets, poultry, or vegetable sticks can be substituted for fish sticks.

Preparation time: 30 min.
Each portion about:
800 calories / 24 g protein
62 g fat / 38 g carbohydrate

Seafood Fondue

4 servings

1 pound 2 ounces (500 g) mixed cleaned seafood (for example, squid, shelled mussels, crabmeat)

4 garlic cloves

3 tablespoons vegetable oil

¼ cup (2 ounces/60 ml) light soy sauce

3 tablespoons lemon juice

1 pound (400 g) raw shelled large shrimp

12 sea scallops (fresh or thawed frozen)

A few lettuce leaves for garnish

3 lemons

1 quart (1 l) vegetable oil for frying

Salt

White pepper

Quick to prepare

1 Rinse seafood and pat dry. Peel and slice garlic. Mix seafood with garlic, oil, soy sauce, and lemon juice. Cover and refrigerate 30 minutes.

2 Rinse shrimp and pat dry. Arrange on lettuce leaves with the scallops and mixed seafood. Cut lemon in wedges and place decoratively on the platters.

3 Heat oil in fondue pot, then set on burner. At the table, spear seafood on fondue forks and fry in hot oil. Season as desired with salt, pepper, and lemon juice.

Other good accompaniments:
Baguette, Curry Cottage Cheese Dip (p. 38), Coconut Rice (p. 43), Remoulade Sauce (p. 59), Lemon Cream (p. 68), and garlic butter or mayonnaise.

Tip: Prepare a batter (p. 75) using wine instead of beer and add to the seafood 1 pound (400 g) fish fillets, cut into bite-size pieces. Serve each diner a small bowl with wine batter. Dip fish and mixed seafood quickly through the batter and fry immediately.

Pour a light, dry white wine or a rosé.

**Preparation time: 30 min.
(+30 min. marinating time)
Each portion about:
530 calories / 44 g protein
35 g fat / 11 g carbohydrate**

4 servings	
FOR THE FONDUE:	
9 ounces (250 g) celery root	
8 ounces (200 g) kohlrabi	
8 ounces (200 g) carrots	
8 ounces (200 g) beets	
8 ounces (200 g) boiling potatoes	
Salt	
3 tablespoons vinegar	
2 tablespoons sesame seeds	
For the Mustard Dip:	
1 cup (8 ounces/200 g) sour cream or crème fraîche	
3 tablespoons sweet prepared mustard	
2 tablespoons lemon juice	
2 shallots	
½ bunch chives	
½ bunch parsley	
Salt	
Black pepper	
1 quart (1 l) vegetable oil for frying	
Vegetarian	

Root Vegetable Fondue

1 Clean, peel, and wash the celery root, kohlrabi, carrots, beets, and potatoes. Cut into 2-inch (5-cm) finger-thick sticks.

2 Bring a pot of well-salted water to boil. Drop in potato sticks and cook 2 to 3 minutes. Lift out with a slotted spoon and drain in a sieve. Bring salted water back to boil. Add celery, kohlrabi, and carrots together and cook 5 minutes or until crisp-tender. Remove vegetables with a slotted spoon, rinse with cold water, and drain well.

3 Add vinegar to the salted water and bring to boil. Add beets, cover, and cook over medium heat until crisp-tender, 15 to 20 minutes.

4 Meanwhile, for the mustard dip, mix the sour cream with the mustard and lemon juice until creamy. Finely chop shallots. Cut chives into fine rings. Finely chop parsley leaves. Stir shallots and herbs into sour cream; season with salt and pepper. Divide sauce among 4 small bowls, place sesame seeds on a plate.

5 Heat oil in the fondue pot on the stove, then set on burner. At the table, spear 1 or 2 vegetable sticks at a time, dunk them in the hot oil, and fry until crisp. Sprinkle as desired with sesame seeds and offer mustard dip. Brown bread or rye bread makes a good accompaniment.

Tip: Homemade Tomato Ketchup (p. 80) is also very good with this vegetable fondue.

Preparation time: 50 min.
Each portion about:
470 calories / 7 g protein
39 g fat / 22 g carbohydrate

8 servings
1 shallot
1 tablespoon drained capers
9 ounces (250 g) ground beef round
1 egg
2 tablespoons dry bread crumbs
1 ounce (25 g) chopped pistachios
Cayenne pepper
Salt / Pepper
11 ounces (300 g) beef fillet
2 garlic cloves
1 teaspoon prepared mustard
2 tablespoons vegetable oil
11 ounces (300 g) pork fillet
1 walnut-size piece fresh ginger
3 tablespoons soy sauce
1 teaspoon Asian chili oil
11 ounces (300 g) turkey breast fillet
3 tablespoons lemon juice
1 teaspoon Worcestershire sauce
6 frankfurters
8 ounces (200 g) shelled and deveined large shrimp
2 tablespoons all-purpose flour
1 quart (1 l) vegetable oil for frying
Lemon wedges for garnish
Low calorie

New Year's Fondue

1 Peel and finely chop shallots. Chop the capers. Mix both with the ground beef, egg, bread crumbs, pistachios, cayenne, salt, and pepper and knead to blend. Shape into small balls and chill until ready to serve.

2 Cut beef fillet into bite-size cubes. Press in garlic and mix in mustard, oil, salt, and pepper.

3 Cut pork fillet into bite-size cubes. Peel ginger and press through a garlic press into the pork. Mix in soy sauce and chili oil.

4 Dice turkey. Mix with lemon juice, Worcestershire sauce, salt, and pepper. Cover and let marinate.

5 Cut frankfurters in pieces and cut a shallow cross into each. Rinse shrimp, pat dry, and roll lightly in flour.

6 Heat oil in fondue pot on the stove, then set on the burner. Arrange all ingredients separately on platters, decorating with lemon wedges. At the table, each diner spears ingredients on a fondue fork and fries them in hot oil. After frying, sprinkle the shrimp with lemon juice.

Other good accompaniments:
Remoulade Sauce (p. 59), Garlic Mayonnaise (p. 43), Lemon Cream (p. 68), and Cocktail Sauce (p. 68).

Tips: Instead of or in addition to frankfurters or sausages, offer 2 generous pounds (1 kg) spareribs, cut into small pieces, in a spicy marinade. For the marinade, combine 5 tablespoons tomato paste, 2 tablespoons each chili sauce and Worcestershire sauce, a little Tabasco, 1 teaspoon sweet paprika, 3 tablespoons vinegar, sugar, salt, and pepper until bubbly. Stir in 2 tablespoons vegetable oil and pour over ribs. Let marinate for 1 day. Drain before frying.

If desired, offer vegetables for frying as well: zucchini, carrots, mushrooms, fennel, and pepper strips are good choices. Also delicious on the side are mixed pickles, pearl onions, small gherkins, baby corn, stuffed olives, a crusty baguette, and an assortment of salads.

Preparation time: 3 hrs. Each portion about: 375 calories 34 g protein / 23 g fat 9 g carbohydrate

Crisp Cheese Fondue

4 servings

1 stale loaf of bread
2 tablespoons cider vinegar
1 tablespoon vegetable oil
5 ounces (125 g) cottage cheese
3 eggs
½ to 1 tablespoon prepared horseradish
5 ounces (125 g) dry bread crumbs
Salt
Pepper
6 ounces (150 g) Bel Paese or other rich, semisoft cheese
6 ounces (150 g) Camembert cheese
2 small Seckel pears
1 tablespoon lemon juice
11 ounces (300 g) red currant or lingonberry preserves
3 tablespoons all-purpose flour
1 quart (1 l) vegetable oil for frying

Vegetarian

1 Trim crusts from bread and cut bread into cubes. Mix with the vinegar and oil and soak 30 minutes. Puree with the cottage cheese. Stir in 1 egg, horseradish, and 3 to 4 tablespoons bread crumbs. Season the mixture with salt and pepper and chill 30 minutes

2 Meanwhile, cut rind from Bel Paese and scrape off the white skin from Camembert. Cut both cheeses into 1-inch (2-cm) cubes. Peel pears, quarter, core, and cut in thin wedges. Immediately sprinkle with lemon juice.

3 Fill small bowls with preserves. Whisk remaining eggs in a shallow dish. Place flour in a second dish and remaining bread crumbs in a third.

4 With damp hands, shape small croquettes of cottage cheese mixture and roll in bread crumbs. Dip the cheese and pear pieces in flour, then in egg, and then in crumbs. Arrange all ingredients decoratively on a platter.

5 Heat oil in fondue pot on the stove, then set on burner. At the table, spear cheese or pear pieces on fondue forks and fry until golden brown. Drop the cheese croquettes into the oil and fry until golden; remove with a fondue strainer. Eat with preserves.

Other good accompaniments:
Almond yogurt is also very good with this fondue. Mix 1 cup (8 ounces/200 g) whole-milk plain yogurt with 1 to 2 tablespoons lemon juice, salt, pepper, and 2 ounces (50 g) blanched toasted almonds, grated.

Preparation time: 1 hr. (+30 min. chilling time) Each portion about: 715 calories / 24 g protein 50 g fat / 43 g carbohydrate

WITH CHEESE

Neuchâtel Fondue

8 ounces (200 g) each Gruyère,
Emmentaler (Swiss), and Freiberg
Vacherin

1-pound (500-g) loaf of white,
sourdough, or onion bread

1 garlic clove

1¼ cups (10 ounces/300 ml) dry
white wine

1 tablespoon cornstarch

6 tablespoons kirsch

Pepper

Freshly grated nutmeg

Lemon juice (optional)

Classic

1 Trim rind from cheese; coarsely grate cheese or cut into small cubes. Cut bread into bite-size cubes.

2 Peel and halve garlic; rub the inside of the fondue pot (*caquelon*) with it. Pour wine into the fondue pot and heat slowly on the stove. Gradually add cheese, stirring constantly in a figure 8 with a wooden spoon. Let cheese melt over low heat, then bring to the bubbling point.

3 Stir cornstarch with kirsch until smooth, pour into cheese, and let bubble. Season with pepper and nutmeg. Stir only until thickened and smooth, stirring in a little lemon juice (if necessary) (see page 19).

4 At the table, keep fondue hot on the burner over a small flame. Have bread ready. Stir the cheese mixture while dipping the bread cubes to keep its consistency creamy.

Other good accompaniments:
Mixed pickles or cornichons.

Special Recipe !

The quality of the cheese will determine the success of any cheese fondue. Without fail, buy it in a good cheese shop. All ingredients can be measured and prepared an hour or two ahead. Cut the bread ahead of time and pack in a plastic bag. Offer mixed pickles on the side. For a beverage, pour black tea or the white wine that was used in the fondue itself.

Preparation time: 40 min.
For 6 persons, each portion
about: 625 calories
35 g protein / 32 g fat
41 g carbohydrate

Farmer's Fondue

6 servings

For the Cabbage Salad:

1 small head cabbage	
4 ounces (100 g) bacon	
2 tablespoons walnut oil	
¼ cup (2 ounces/60 ml) cider vinegar	
Salt	
Pepper	
1 sour apple	
2 tablespoons lemon juice	
2 ounces (50 g) walnut meats	

FOR THE FONDUE:

11 ounces (300 g) seeded dark bread	
9 ounces (250 g) small mushrooms	
11 ounces (300 g) Emmentaler	
11 ounces (300 g) mountain cheese	
4 ounces (125 g) bacon	
1 tablespoon butter	
1¼ cups (10 ounces/300 ml) hard cider or dry apple wine	
2 tablespoons lemon juice	
1 tablespoon cornstarch	
6 tablespoons Calvados or apple brandy	
Pepper	
2 bunches chives	

Economical

1 For the salad, trim the cabbage and cut crosswise into thin strips or grate. In a bowl, pour boiling water over and let stand 2 minutes. Drain and press firmly.

2 Dice bacon very fine. Fry over medium heat until crisp, then pour off fat. Add bacon, oil, vinegar, salt, and pepper to the cabbage. Core apple and cut into fine julienne. Sprinkle at once with lemon juice to prevent darkening. Chop walnuts. Fold the apples and walnuts into the cabbage.

3 For the fondue, dice bread into bite-size cubes. Wipe mushrooms clean. Remove rind from cheese and grate cheese. Dice bacon very fine.

4 Melt butter in a saucepan and fry bacon in it over medium heat until crisp. Pour off excess fat. Gradually pour in apple cider and lemon juice and heat. Gradually add cheese, stirring in a figure 8 over low heat.

5 Stir cornstarch with Calvados, pour into fondue, and bring to boil. Season with pepper. Cut chives into very fine rings; stir into fondue. Pour into fondue pot and set hot on burner, having the other ingredients ready. At the table, dip the bread and mushrooms into the cheese mixture.

Other good accompaniments:
Salad, radishes, and spicy gherkins.

Preparation time: 1 hr. Each portion about: 930 calories 39 g protein / 67 g fat 33 g carbohydrate

6 servings

For the Dandelion Salad:

9 ounces (250 g) boiling potatoes

4 ounces (100 g) cooked ham

1 onion

1 garlic clove

Salt

Pepper

1 teaspoon sharp prepared mustard

3 tablespoons wine vinegar

5 tablespoons oil

1 to 2 bunches pale (blanched) dandelion greens or Belgian endive (about 8 ounces/200 g)

FOR THE FONDUE:

1 pound 2 ounces (500 g) mixed white and dark bread

2 sticks (8 ounces/200 g) butter

14 ounces (350 g) Emmentaler cheese

8 egg yolks

White pepper

Freshly grated nutmeg

$\frac{2}{3}$ cup (5 ounces/125 g) heavy cream

2 tablespoons dry white wine or lemon juice

Classic

Geneva Fondue

1 For the dandelion salad, wash potatoes and cook unpeeled in a little water for 15 to 20 minutes until just tender. Drain and let cool a little, then peel and slice. Cut ham into small cubes.

2 Chop the onion and force the garlic into it through a press. Mix in a large bowl with salt, pepper, mustard, and vinegar, then whisk in the oil.

3 Wash dandelion greens and shake dry. Cut off tough stems and cut the leaves into wide strips. Toss with the potatoes and ham and carefully fold in dressing.

4 Cut bread into bite-size cubes. In a wide skillet, heat about $\frac{1}{2}$ stick (2 ounces/50 g) butter until foamy. Add bread cubes and sauté until golden brown on all sides. Remove from the pan and set aside.

5 Remove rind from Emmentaler and grate finely. Mix with the egg yolks in a fondue pot (*caquelon*) and season with pepper, nutmeg, and a little salt. Place the pot on the stove at the lowest heat and gradually add the remaining butter in small pieces, stirring constantly. Do not boil.

6 When the mixture is thick and smooth, pour in cream and the wine or lemon juice and stir in quickly. Set on the burner but never let it boil. Spear bread on forks and pull through the cheese mixture. Eat with dandelion salad.

Tip: If the fondue on the burner accidentally boils and the egg yolk curdles, immediately stir in some lemon juice.

Preparation time: 1 hr.
Each portion about:
970 calories / 33 g protein
70 g fat / 52 g carbohydrate

Waadtländer Fondue

4 to 6 servings

1 pound 5 ounces (600 g) Gruyère cheese of different ages (3 different ones, if possible)
1 garlic clove
1-pound 2-ounce (500-g) baguette and/or other crusty bread
1 teaspoon butter
1⅓ cups (11 ounces/300 ml) dry white wine (Waadtländer, Neuchâtel, or German Boxbeutel)
1 teaspoon lemon juice
1 tablespoon cornstarch
¼ cup (2 ounces/60 ml) kirsch
Freshly grated nutmeg
White pepper

Classic

1 Trim rind from cheese and grate coarsely. Finely chop garlic. Cut bread into bite-size cubes.

2 Melt butter in fondue pot (*caquelon*) on the stove over medium heat and sauté garlic lightly. Pour in the wine and lemon juice and heat. Gradually add the cheese, stirring constantly, and let melt over low heat. Always stir in a figure 8, so the cheese does not form strings.

3 Mix the cornstarch with the kirsch and stir into the hot cheese mixture. Season with nutmeg and pepper. Bring to boil, then keep the fondue hot on the burner without further boiling. At the table, spear bread cubes on fondue forks and pull through the hot cheese mixture, stirring the cheese as you dip.

Tips: This fondue is prepared from Gruyère of several different ages; you will need to purchase it in a good cheese shop.

Delicious additions are finely chopped fresh herbs such as lovage, tarragon, parsley, or rosemary.

Garlic lovers can mix 2 to 3 pressed cloves and a few garlic slices into the cheese mixture. Garlic makes the cheese a little easier to digest.

Preparation time: 1 hr. For 6 persons, each portion about:
690 calories / 37 g protein
33 g fat / 2 g carbohydrate

Fondue with Dutch Cheese

1 Peel and halve the garlic and carefully rub the fondue pot (*caquelon*) with it. Trim crusts from all the cheeses and grate coarsely on a vegetable grater or with a food processor.

2 Mix the wine and lemon juice in the fondue pot and warm. Gradually add grated cheese, stirring constantly in a figure 8 with a wooden spoon over low heat until wine and cheese have combined into a smooth mixture.

3 Mix the cornstarch and port until smooth and stir well into the cheese. Heat again, stirring. Set on the burner, season with pepper and nutmeg, and keep hot, stirring occasionally.

4 Cut bread into 1-inch (2-cm) cubes and either toast in a dry skillet or serve fresh. Spear the bread on fondue forks and draw through the cheese mixture. Eat with ham.

Tips: Instead of bread, offer thickly sliced warm potatoes, cooked carrots, or parsnips. Or accompany the fondue with fresh vegetable sticks—carrots, cucumber, celery, green onions—and sour apple slices.

If you cannot get the recommended cheese varieties, you can use Gouda of several ages and season the mixture with ground cumin.

Pour a dry, crisp white wine or an aromatic black tea and shot glasses of Genever, a Dutch juniper-flavored gin.

Preparation time: 40 min.
For 6 persons, each portion
about: 840 calories
41 g protein / 50 g fat
2 g carbohydrate

Cheese Fondue with Mushrooms

4 to 6 servings

10 ounces (300 g) mixed fresh mushrooms
1 onion
1 tablespoon butter
½ bunch parsley
Salt
Pepper
8 ounces (200 g) Gruyère cheese
8 ounces (200 g) raclette cheese
8 ounces (200 g) Swiss Emmentaler cheese
3 to 4 teaspoons cornstarch
1 pound 2 ounces (500 g) fresh pumpernickel
1 garlic clove
1¼ cups (10 ounces/300 ml) dry white wine
1 tablespoon lemon juice
2 tablespoons kirsch
Freshly grated nutmeg
Sweet paprika

Vegetarian

1 Clean mushrooms, slice thinly. Finely chop the onion and sauté in the butter until translucent. Add mushrooms and sauté over medium heat 5 minutes. The excess mushroom liquid should evaporate.

2 Tear off parsley leaves and chop finely. Remove mushrooms from heat. Mix in parsley and season with salt and pepper.

3 Trim rind from cheese and grate cheese coarsely. Toss with cornstarch. Cut the bread into cubes and place in a bowl.

4 Peel and halve garlic. Place a fondue pot (*caquelon*) on the stove and rub well with the garlic. Pour in the wine and lemon juice and heat slowly over low heat.

5 Gradually add cheese mixture and let it melt slowly, stirring in a figure 8 (this will take 10 to 15 minutes). Stir in the kirsch. Season with salt, pepper, nutmeg, and paprika. Add the mushroom mixture.

6 Set the pot on the burner and let the fondue simmer over low heat. Spear bread cubes on skewers and pull through the cheese mixture.

Tip: As another accompaniment you can offer the bright green of green onions, cut into strips.

Serve with a dry Italian white wine, for example a Galestro from Tuscany. You can use it in the fondue as well.

Preparation time: 50 min.
For 6 persons, each portion
about: 660 calories
36 g protein / 35 g fat
39 g carbohydrate

Cheese Fondue with Tomatoes

4 to 6 servings

2 pounds (800 g) mixed vegetables (fennel, tender carrots, shallots, broccoli florets, red and yellow bell peppers)

Salt

11 ounces (300 g) firm white bread

1 pound 2 ounces (500 g) tomatoes

8 ounces (200 g) Gruyère cheese

8 ounces (200 g) Appenzeller cheese

8 ounces (200 g) mountain cheese

1 onion

1 garlic clove

2 tablespoons butter

1½ cups (12 ounces/⅜ l) dry white wine

3 tablespoons tomato paste

1 tablespoon cornstarch

1 teaspoon lemon juice

Pepper

1 teaspoon chopped fresh oregano

Vegetarian

1 Clean and trim all vegetables and cut into bite-size pieces. Leave small carrots whole. One after another, blanch in boiling salted water: fennel, carrots, and shallots 5 minutes, broccoli florets 3 minutes. Drain vegetables, rinse with ice water and drain well. Leave pepper pieces raw. Arrange vegetables decoratively on a platter. Cut bread into cubes and place in a bowl.

2 Core tomatoes. Dip tomatoes in boiling water briefly, then skin and quarter. Seed tomatoes and chop finely. Trim rind from cheeses and grate coarsely.

3 Finely chop onion and garlic. Melt butter in a fondue pot (*caquelon*) over low heat and sauté onion and garlic until translucent. Add tomatoes and sauté, stirring, 2 minutes. Pour in all but ¼ cup (2 ounces/60 ml) of the wine, stir in tomato paste, and heat, stirring, on the stove. Gradually add cheese and let melt, stirring constantly in a figure 8 over low heat. When cheese is melted, raise heat and bring to boil.

4 Whisk cornstarch with reserved wine and lemon juice. Stir into cheese mixture and return to boil. Season with pepper and oregano.

5 Set pot on the fondue burner, regulating heat so that the mixture simmers very gently. At the table, each guest spears a piece of bread or vegetable on his fork and dips it into the hot fondue.

Pour a dry white wine or a chilled rosé.

Preparation time: 1 hr.
For 6 persons, each portion
about: 685 calories
37 g protein / 37 g fat
39 g carbohydrate

Spicy Cheese Fondue

4 to 6 servings

9 ounces (250 g) small boiling potatoes
8 ounces (200 g) small firm mushrooms
1 small loaf onion bread (9 ounces/250 g)
1 can baby corn (1 pound/400 g)
1 large pear
2 tablespoons lemon juice
1 small red chili pepper
1 small green chili pepper
1 garlic clove
9 ounces (250 g) Emmentaler cheese
9 ounces (250 g) Gruyère cheese
2 cups (16 ounces/500 ml) dry white wine
1½ tablespoons cornstarch
5 tablespoons kirsch

Economical

1 Wash potatoes and cook unpeeled in a little water 15 to 20 minutes or until just cooked. Drain and cool somewhat, then peel.

2 Wipe mushrooms and cut large ones in half. Cut bread into bite-size cubes. Drain corn. Quarter and core the pear; cut quarters across in 1-inch (2-cm) slices. Immediately sprinkle with lemon juice.

3 Slit chilies, seed, and finely chop. Peel garlic and force through a garlic press.

4 Trim rind from cheeses and grate cheese coarsely. Slowly warm the wine in a fondue pot (*caquelon*) on the stove, adding chilies and garlic.

5 Gradually add cheese over low heat, stirring constantly with a wooden spoon in a figure 8. When cheese is melted, bring just to boil.

6 Stir cornstarch with kirsch until smooth and pour into cheese mixture. Stir until the mixture is thickened and creamy. Set on a burner with a small flame. At the table, spear potato, vegetable, pear, and bread on forks and pull through the hot fondue.

Preparation time: 45 min.
For 6 persons, each portion about:
635 calories / 31 g protein
28 g fat / 45 g carbohydrate

Beer Cheese Fondue

4 to 6 servings

11 ounces (300 g) Gruyère cheese
11 ounces (300 g) Emmentaler cheese
1 teaspoon caraway seeds
1 teaspoon coriander seeds
1 pound 2 ounces (500 g) bread (a mixture of baguette, crusty bread, and soft pretzels)
1 cup (8 ounces/250 ml) light beer
1 tablespoon cornstarch
Pepper
1 garlic clove
2 tablespoons kümmel (caraway liqueur) or kirsch

Economical

1 Trim crusts from cheeses and grate coarsely. Finely crush the caraway and coriander seeds in a mortar. Cut bread and soft pretzels into bite-size cubes.

2 Heat beer in fondue pot (*caquelon*) over low heat. Stir in a handful of cheese and melt, stirring constantly. Gradually add remaining cheese, continuing to stir in a figure 8.

3 Whisk the cornstarch with 2 tablespoons cold water and stir into cheese. Season cheese with caraway, coriander, and pepper. Peel garlic and force through a press into cheese. Bring mixture just to boil, stirring, and set on fondue burner. Just before serving, stir in kümmel. Spear bread on fondue forks and pull through the hot cheese.

Other good accompaniments:
Small boiled potatoes (with skin so cheese will adhere better), cubed sausage, liverwurst, or cooked ham, small gherkins, pearl onions, baby corn, mixed pickles, pickled watermelon rind, radishes, radicchio salad, and tomato salad.

Pour chilled beer.

Preparation time: 1 hr.
For 6 persons, each portion
about: 645 calories
36 g protein / 32 g fat
3 g carbohydrate

Quick Cheese Bacon Fondue

4 to 6 servings

9 ounces (250 g) raclette cheese
9 ounces (250 g) chèvre cheese
9 ounces (250 g)
Appenzeller cheese
4 ounces (100 g) bacon
1 tablespoon cornstarch
½ cup (4 ounces/125 ml)
dry white wine
1 pound 2 ounces (500 g)
bread (baguette, onion bread,
and/or herb bread)
1 tablespoon vegetable oil
1 garlic clove
1 teaspoon dried marjoram
½ teaspoon sweet paprika
¼ cup (2 ounces/60 ml) kirsch

Easy

1 Trim rind from cheese if necessary and cut in small cubes. Finely dice bacon. Stir cornstarch with white wine. Cut bread into bite-size cubes.

2 Heat oil in fondue pot (*caquelon*) on the stove and brown bacon cubes over moderate heat. Add cheese cubes bit by bit, stirring constantly; the cheese will clump at first, then melt. When all cheese is melted, stir in the wine mixture. Peel garlic and force through press into cheese, stirring in a figure 8 so cheese does not get stringy.

3 Season cheese mixture with marjoram and paprika and set on the burner. Just before serving, stir in kirsch. At the table, spear bread cubes on a fondue fork and pull it through the hot cheese mixture.

Other good accompaniments:
Salami rolls, sausage cubes, blanched cauliflower and broccoli florets, small mushroom caps, olives, mustard pickles, small meatballs (p. 70), and Potato Lettuce Salad (p. 74).

Pour a good chilled Pilsner.

Preparation time: 1¼ hrs.
For 6 persons, each portion
about: 615 calories
27 g protein / 30 g fat
2 g carbohydrate

4 servings

2 pounds (1 kg) very
small boiling potatoes
9 ounces (250 g) medium-
aged Gouda cheese
1 pound (400 g) mushrooms
2 tablespoons butter
2 cups (16 ounces/400 g)
heavy cream
1 tablespoon cornstarch
¼ cup (2 ounces/50 ml) vegetable
broth
1 large bunch parsley
Salt
2 teaspoons lemon juice
1 tablespoon dry sherry
or white port
White pepper
Pinch of cayenne pepper
Parsley leaves for garnish

Vegetarian

Mushroom Cheese Fondue

1 Wash potatoes well and cook covered, in a little water, until just cooked. Peel and keep warm.

2 Meanwhile, trim rind from cheese and finely grate cheese on a vegetable grater or in the food processor. Wipe mushrooms or rinse quickly in a sieve and pat dry. Chop coarsely.

3 In a fondue pot (*caquelon*) melt butter over medium heat on the stove. Sauté mushrooms until excess liquid evaporates.

4 Pour in cream and simmer over medium heat 3 minutes. Mix cornstarch with broth until smooth, stir into cream mixture, and bring to boil. Finely chop parsley leaves.

5 Gradually add cheese to cream sauce, stirring in a figure 8, and let melt over low heat. Lightly heat the fondue again, seasoning with parsley, salt, lemon juice, sherry or port, pepper, and cayenne. Set on a burner and garnish with parsley leaves. Serve potatoes with the fondue. At the table, each diner takes potatoes on his plate and covers them with the hot cheese-mushroom mixture. Serve with bread.

Tips: Instead of potatoes you can also serve the fondue with bread cubes.

This is tasty with a tossed salad or with steamed spinach or beet greens sautéed with butter, minced onion, and a little garlic.

Preparation time: 1 hr.
Each portion about:
800 calories / 24 g protein
56 g fat / 48 g carbohydrate

Cream Cheese Fondue

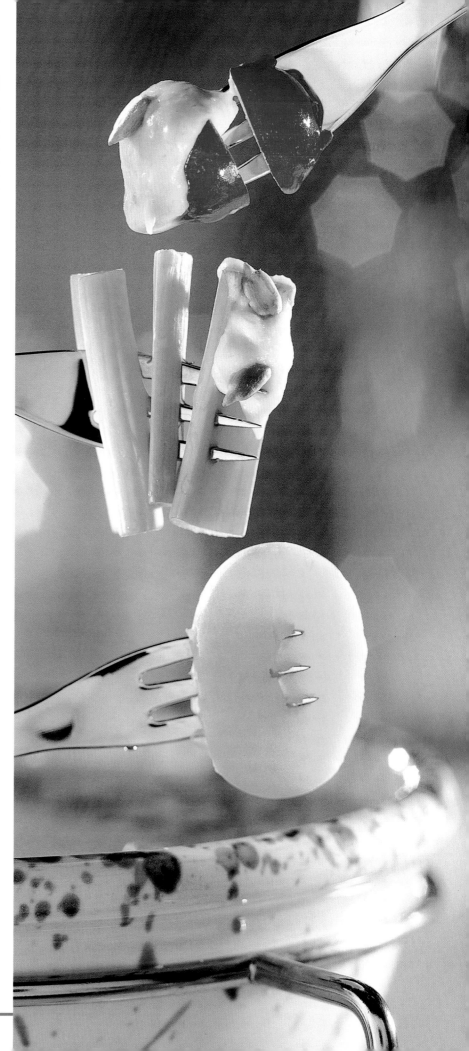

4 to 6 servings

2 pounds (1 kg) small boiling potatoes
2 tablespoons sunflower seeds
11 ounces (300 g) Emmentaler cheese
1 bunch radishes
1 bunch green onions
2 shallots
1 garlic clove
1 bunch mixed fresh herbs
(parsley, chives, dill, basil, tarragon)
2 tablespoons butter
$1\frac{1}{2}$ cups (12 ounces/$\frac{3}{8}$ l)
vegetable broth
11 ounces (300 g) cream cheese
1 heaping teaspoon cornstarch
2 tablespoons lemon juice
$\frac{1}{4}$ cup (2 ounces/50 g) heavy cream
Salt / Pepper
Hot paprika

Economical

1 Wash the potatoes and cook, covered, in a little water 15 to 20 minutes until just cooked.

2 Meanwhile, roast the sunflower seeds in a dry skillet over medium heat. Let cool somewhat and chop. Trim rind from the Emmentaler and grate finely.

3 Clean and halve radishes. Trim green onion and cut into $1\frac{1}{2}$-inch (4-cm) pieces, halving the white parts lengthwise. Peel potatoes if desired, then cut in thick slices. Arrange all ingredients decoratively on a platter.

4 Finely chop shallots and garlic. Finely chop herbs.

5 Heat the butter in a pot and sauté the shallots and garlic until translucent. Pour in broth and heat. Add the Emmentaler and the cream cheese and stir constantly over low heat just until mixture bubbles.

6 Mix the cornstarch with the lemon juice and stir into the fondue. Stir in the cream, chopped herbs, and sunflower seeds. Season with salt, pepper, and paprika. Pour the cheese mixture into the fondue pot (*caquelon*) and set on the burner. Serve potatoes, radishes, and green onion for dipping.

Other good accompaniments:
Instead of potatoes, serve cubes of different bread varieties, for example rye bread, white bread sticks, whole wheat bread, and pumpernickel.

Preparation time: 1 hr. For 6 persons, each portion about:
595 calories / 23 g protein
39 g fat / 38 g carbohydrate

1 can (1 pound/400 g)
artichoke hearts
1 tablespoon red wine vinegar
4 tablespoons lemon juice
Salt
Black pepper
1/4 cup (2 ounces/60 ml) extra virgin
olive oil
1/2 bunch parsley
5 ounces (150 g) small mushrooms
1 loaf Italian bread
8 ounces (200 g) beef fillet
1 tablespoon clarified butter
5 ounces (150 g) marinated bottled
red pepper strips
5 ounces (150 g) rigatoni
1 garlic clove
11 ounces (300 g) provolone cheese
11 ounces (300 g) Gorgonzola,
Cambozola, or other blue cheese
1 cup (8 ounces/200 g) heavy
cream
1 cup (8 ounces/250 ml) dry white
wine
4 teaspoons cornstarch
2 tablespoons grappa

Easy

Gorgonzola Provolone Fondue

1 Drain and quarter the artichoke hearts. Whisk the vinegar, 2 tablespoons lemon juice, salt, pepper, and olive oil. Finely chop parsley leaves and stir into the marinade. Fold in artichoke hearts and chill.

2 Wipe mushrooms and sprinkle with the remaining lemon juice. Cut bread into cubes. Pepper the fillet and sauté in hot clarified butter until browned on all sides. Remove from heat and season with salt. Cover and let rest until partially cooled, then cut in thin slices. Arrange decoratively on a platter with the mushrooms and red pepper strips. Cook rigatoni in plenty of salted water 10 minutes or until al dente.

3 Meanwhile, peel and halve garlic and rub the fondue pot (*caquelon*) with it. Finely dice both varieties of cheese and add to the pot with the cream. Pour in all but 3 tablespoons of the wine. Stir constantly over low heat until the cheese is melted.

4 Whisk the reserved wine with the cornstarch and stir into the cheese mixture. Set the fondue on the burner and stir in grappa and pepper.

5 Drain noodles well and transfer to a warmed bowl. Place the bread and marinated artichokes in bowls. Spear the rigatoni, bread cubes, mushrooms, and meat on skewers and pull through the cheese mixture. Eat with the artichokes and the red pepper strips.

Tip: For extra zest, stir 2 ounces (50 g) finely diced dried tomatoes into the cheese mixture shortly before serving.

Preparation time: 50 min.
For 6 persons, each portion
about: 795 calories
38 g protein / 53 g fat
23 g carbohydrate

Cheese Tortellini Fondue

4 to 6 servings

For the Arugula Salad:

4 tablespoons pine nuts
2 firm tomatoes
4 ounces (100 g) shallots
Salt
Pepper
¼ cup (2 ounces/60 ml) balsamic vinegar
2 teaspoons honey
6 tablespoons olive oil
8 ounces (200 g) arugula

FOR THE FONDUE:

Salt
11 ounces (300 g) fresh tortellini
8 shelled and deveined cooked shrimp
5 ounces (150 g) cherry tomatoes
1 package thin, crisp bread sticks (grissini)
2 tablespoons lemon juice
1 cup (8 ounces/250 ml) milk
11 ounces (300 g) blue cheese
11 ounces (300 g) fontina cheese
Pepper
1 bunch fresh basil

Quick to prepare

1 For the arugula salad, toast the pine nuts in a dry skillet over medium heat until golden; set aside. Quarter and seed tomatoes. Remove cores and dice the flesh.

2 Finely chop the shallots. Place in a large bowl with the salt, pepper, vinegar, and honey, and whisk in oil. Trim the arugula and remove the coarse stems. Cut into bite-size pieces and fold into the dressing. Sprinkle with tomatoes and pine nuts.

3 For the fondue, bring salted water to boil in a pot. Cook tortellini until al dente, then drain and cool under water, to stop cooking.

4 Rinse the shrimp with cold water and pat dry. Sprinkle with lemon juice. Have cherry tomatoes and bread sticks ready.

5 Warm the milk in the fondue pot (*caquelon*). Dice blue cheese and add to milk, stirring until melted. Dice the fontina, add, and stir until melted. Season with pepper. Cut basil leaves into julienne and stir into the cheese mixture. Set on a burner over a low flame. At the table, draw tortellini, tomatoes, and shrimp through the cheese mixture; dunk bread sticks. Serve the arugula salad alongside.

Pour a dry white wine.

Preparation time: 40 min.
For 6 persons, each portion
about: 830 calories
41 g protein / 51 g fat
45 g carbohydrate

For the Smoked Salmon Tartare:

2 ounces (50 g) shallots
1 bunch dill
1 bunch parsley
8 ounces (200 g) smoked salmon
2 tablespoons lemon juice
Salt
White pepper
1 tablespoon sour cream
1 tablespoon walnut oil

FOR THE FONDUE:

1 pound 2 ounces (500 g) leeks
Salt
1 pound (400 g) rye bread
1 pound 4 ounces (600 g) cheddar cheese
1 cup (8 ounces/250 ml) Guinness stout
4 teaspoons cornstarch
2 tablespoons whiskey
Pepper
A few dashes of Worcestershire sauce
Dill sprigs for garnish

Easy

Irish Fondue

1 For the salmon tartare, finely chop shallots. Chop the dill and the parsley. Finely dice the salmon and mix with shallots, dill, parsley, lemon juice, salt, white pepper, sour cream, and walnut oil.

2 For the fondue, trim the leeks, wash well, and shake dry. Cut into bite-size pieces. Bring lightly salted water to boil and blanch the leeks for 3 minutes. Drain well. Cut the rye bread into bite-size cubes. Arrange with the leeks.

3 Cut the cheese into very small cubes or grate coarsely. Lightly heat the beer in a fondue pot (*caquelon*) on the stove. Gradually add cheese and melt over low heat, stirring constantly (this will take 30 to 35 minutes).

4 Stir the cornstarch with the whiskey, pour into cheese, and bring to boil, stirring. Season the mixture with pepper and Worcestershire sauce and set the fondue burner, holding it just at the boiling point. Garnish with dill sprigs. Spear leeks and bread pieces on fondue forks and draw through the cheese mixture. Offer smoked salmon tartare alongside.

Serve with beer—naturally, an Irish brew would be best.

Preparation time: 1 hr.
For 6 persons, each portion about: 720 calories
41 g protein / 42 g fat
39 g carbohydrate

Dill Fondue

4 servings

1 pound 2 ounces (500 g)
boiling potatoes
2 tablespoons butter
10 ounces (250 g) Bauernbrot
(dark bread)
8 ounces (200 g) shelled and
deveined cooked shrimp
Pepper
2 tablespoons lemon juice
1 pound 2 ounces (500 g) Havarti
or Tilsiter cheese
1¼ cups (10 ounces/300 ml)
dry white wine
1 tablespoon cornstarch
1 tablespoon kümmel (caraway liqueur)
2 bunches dill

Economical

1 Wash the potatoes and boil unpeeled in a little water 15 to 20 minutes or until just cooked. Drain and let cool a little, then peel and cut into coarse cubes. Heat the butter in a nonstick pan until foamy and cook potatoes in it until golden brown on all sides. Set aside.

2 Dice the bread into bite-size cubes. Rinse the shrimp with cold water and pat dry. Season with pepper and lemon juice. Arrange bread, potatoes, and shrimp on platters.

3 Cut the cheese into small cubes. Warm the wine in the fondue pot (*caquelon*) on the stove, gradually add the Havarti, and stir over low heat until melted. Stir the cornstarch with the kümmel until smooth, pour into cheese, and bring just to boil, stirring.

4 Chop the dill and stir into the cheese mixture. Keep hot on fondue burner over a low flame. At the table, spear potatoes, bread, and shrimp on fondue forks and draw through the cheese mixture.

Preparation time: 1 hr. Each portion about: 880 calories 56 g protein / 44 g fat 50 g carbohydrate

Fonduta with Truffles

4 servings

11 ounces (300 g) fontina cheese
(or use provolone or another
Italian slicing cheese with at
least 40% fat)
1 cup (8 ounces/250 ml) milk
1 loaf Italian bread
(or baguette)
5 tablespoons butter
3 egg yolks
2 tablespoons heavy cream
White pepper
1 fresh truffle, preferably
white (or 1 black truffle or firm
porcini mushroom)

Specialty from Italy

1 Trim rind from cheese and cut into very small cubes. Place in a large bowl, pour milk over, and let soak, uncovered, 4 to 6 hours.

2 Just before proceeding, cut the bread into bite-size pieces. Melt 2 tablespoons of the butter in a large pan and sauté bread cubes in it until crisp on all sides. Keep warm in the oven at low setting until serving time.

3 Prepare a double boiler. Place the cheese mixture in the top and warm over low heat, whisking constantly, until cheese is melted.

4 Whisk egg yolks with cream and stir into the cheese in a thin stream; do not boil or the egg yolks will curdle. Chop remaining butter into small flakes and gradually stir into the cheese mixture. Continue stirring with a wooden spoon until the cheese no longer forms any strings. Transfer fondue to the fondue pot, season with pepper, and keep warm at the table (ideally on a hot plate). Wipe the truffle clean; if necessary, rub off any remaining dirt with a soft brush.

5 At the table, have everyone ladle some of the fondue into a small bowl and shave the truffle in paper thin slices (a special truffle plane is best for this). Spear bread pieces on forks and dunk in the fondue.

**Preparation time: 1½ hrs.
(about 4–6 hrs. soaking time)
Each portion about:
765 calories / 26 g protein
59 g fat / 6 g carbohydrate**

Goat Cheese Fondue

4 to 6 servings

2 pounds (800 g) broccoli

Salt

3 tablespoons
white wine vinegar

1 tablespoon balsamic vinegar

Pepper

6 tablespoons extra
virgin olive oil

1 shallot

5 ounces (150 g) dried
tomatoes in oil

1 baguette

11 ounces (300 g)
raclette cheese

11 ounces (300 g) semi-soft
garlic cheese

11 ounces (300 g) chèvre cheese

1 garlic clove

1¼ cups (10 ounces/300 ml)
dry white wine

2 teaspoons cornstarch

¼ cup (2 ounces/60 ml) grappa

Freshly grated nutmeg

Pinch of cayenne pepper

Quick to prepare

1 The day before serving, trim broccoli and cut off florets. Cook in plenty of rapidly boiling salted water 2 to 3 minutes or until crisp-tender. Drain (reserving the cooking liquid), rinse with cold water, and drain well again.

2 Whisk both vinegars, ½ cup (4 ounces/125 ml) of the broccoli cooking water, salt, pepper, and olive oil. Finely chop the shallots and stir in. Fold in the broccoli and chill, covered, overnight.

3 The next day, drain the dried tomatoes, cut in small strips, and place in a small bowl. Cut bread into bite-size cubes and place in a bowl. Trim rinds from all three cheeses and cut cheese into small cubes.

4 Peel and halve the garlic; rub fondue pot (*caquelon*) with it. Add the cheese and wine and melt the cheese, stirring constantly, over medium heat.

5 Mix cornstarch with grappa and stir into the cheese mixture. Cook 2 to 3 minutes or until mixture is thickened. Season with pepper, nutmeg, and cayenne.

6 Set the pot on the burner and bring the cheese mixture back to boil. Spear the broccoli florets, dried tomatoes, and bread on fondue forks and draw through the cheese mixture.

Tip: Boiled potatoes can be substituted for bread in this hearty cheese fondue. Use 1 pound 2 ounces (500 g), cooked, peeled, and cubed.

Pour a chilled Chardonnay.

*Preparation time: 30 min.
(+12 hrs. marinating time) For
6 persons, each portion about:
785 calories / 39 g protein
53 g fat / 20 g carbohydrate*

4 to 6 servings

11 ounces (300 g) whole
wheat bread

2 tablespoons butter

2 small, firm pears (for
example, Bosc)

1 sour green apple

3 tablespoons lemon juice

2 to 3 small Belgian endive
(11 ounces/300 g)

4 ounces (100 g) Bündnerfleisch
(air-dried beef) or thinly
sliced prosciutto

1 garlic clove

11 ounces (300 g) Roquefort or
other blue cheese

11 ounces (300 g) Gruyère cheese

11 ounces (300 g) vacherin cheese

4 teaspoons cornstarch

1½ cups (12 ounces/350 ml) hard
cider or apple wine

2 tablespoons pear brandy

Pepper

Cayenne pepper

Quick to prepare

Blue Cheese Fondue

1 Cut bread into large cubes. Melt butter in a pan and sauté bread cubes in it, over medium heat, stirring, until golden brown. Cool and place in a bowl.

2 Quarter, peel, and core pears and apple. Cut quarters into smaller wedges and immediately sprinkle with 2 tablespoons lemon juice. Trim endive, halve lengthwise, and cut core out in a wedge shape. Separate endive into single leaves and cut these into bite-size pieces. Arrange the apple and pear wedges, endive, and meat on plates.

3 Peel and halve the garlic; rub the fondue pot (*caquelon*) with it. Cut the Roquefort into cubes. Grate the Gruyère and vacherin. Mix the three cheeses in the fondue pot with the cornstarch, cider, and remaining lemon juice and bring to boil, stirring, until cheese is melted. Add the pear brandy, pepper, and a pinch of cayenne pepper.

4 Set the fondue on the burner. At the table, spear the bread, apple, pear, and endive on skewers and draw through the cheese mixture. Stir occasionally in a figure 8 so the fondue does not congeal. Eat with the meat.

Tip: At the end, mix 2 ounces (50 g) finely chopped walnuts into the remaining cheese mixture.

Pour white wine or the same cider used in the fondue.

*Preparation time: 30 min.
For 6 persons, each portion
about: 800 calories
47 g protein / 46 g fat
49 g carbohydrate*

Feta Cheese Fondue

4 to 6 servings

1 pound 2 ounces (500 g) small yellow summer squash
2 tablespoons olive oil / Salt / Pepper
1 teaspoon dried thyme
3 to 4 tablespoons lemon juice
1 pound (400 g) cucumbers
11 ounces (300 g) tomatoes
5 ounces (150 g) black olives
1 pound 2 ounces (500 g) sesame flatbread
1 pound (400 g) mild feta cheese
1 garlic clove
¼ cup (2 ounces/50 g) butter
11 ounces (300 g) cream cheese
1 cup (8 ounces/250 ml) milk
1 heaping teaspoon cornstarch
Hot paprika
1 teaspoon chopped fresh oregano
6 large basil leaves

Economical

1 Trim the squash and shave in thin slices. Heat the olive oil and sauté a few squash slices at a time for 5 minutes over medium heat until golden brown. Season with salt, pepper, thyme, and 2 tablespoons of the lemon juice.

2 Peel the cucumbers, quarter lengthwise, and cut diagonally in pieces. Cut tomatoes into eighths. Pit olives. Cube bread. Decoratively arrange the cucumbers, tomatoes, olives, and bread on plates.

3 Coarsely grate the feta. Peel and halve the garlic and rub the fondue pot (*caquelon*) well with it. Mix the butter, feta, and cream cheese in the fondue pot. Stir in all but ¼ cup (2 ounces/ 60 ml) of the milk. Heat the mixture slowly over low heat, stirring constantly, until the cheese melts.

4 Mix the cornstarch with the reserved milk. Stir into the fondue and bring to boil, boiling until mixture thickens. Season with paprika, oregano, and 1 to 2 tablespoons lemon juice.

5 Cut the basil leaves into julienne and sprinkle over the squash. Set the fondue on the burner. At the table, let fondue simmer over a low flame. Draw the flatbread, tomatoes, cucumbers, and olives through the cheese mixture. Eat with summer squash.

Pour a chilled, fresh white wine, such as Pinot Grigio, or a light rosé.

Preparation time: 45 min. For 6 persons, each portion about: 730 calories / 24 g protein 41 g fat / 58 g carbohydrate

Apple Nut Fondue

4 to 6 servings

1 pound 2 ounces (500 g) Brie
(40% to 50% fat content, not
completely ripened)
1 small onion
1 sour green apple
4 tablespoons lemon juice
1 pound 2 ounces (500 g)
crusty bread
2 tablespoons butter
1 cup (8 ounces/250 ml)
apple juice
1 tablespoon cornstarch
White pepper
Salt
1 teaspoon prepared mustard
¼ teaspoon sweet paprika
Freshly grated nutmeg
4 ounces (100 g) walnuts, chopped
¼ cup (2 ounces/60 ml)
Calvados or apple brandy

Vegetarian

1 Cut rind off the Brie and finely cube the cheese. Finely chop the onion. Peel and core apple, grate coarsely, and sprinkle with 1 tablespoon lemon juice. Cut bread into bite-size cubes.

2 Melt the butter in a fondue pot on the stove over medium heat and sauté the onion and apple until tender. Pour in the apple juice and bring to simmer. Gradually add cheese, stirring constantly over low heat. Keep stirring in a figure 8 until cheese is melted.

3 Mix the cornstarch with the remaining lemon juice and stir into the cheese mixture. Season with white pepper, salt, mustard, paprika, and nutmeg. Stir in the nuts and Calvados and keep the fondue hot on the burner. At the table, spear bread cubes on fondue forks and draw through the hot cheese mixture.

Other good accompaniments:
Pear wedges, cooked small potatoes, ham rolls, mushrooms, broccoli florets (cooked until crisp-tender), and a few walnut halves for garnish.

Pour a dry white wine or hard cider.

Preparation time: 1 hr.
For 6 persons, each portion
about: 685 calories
27 g protein / 36 g fat
14 g carbohydrate

Chicken Curry Fondue

4 to 6 servings

1 pound 2 ounces (500 g) skinless, boneless chicken breasts

Salt

Pepper

¼ cup (2 ounces/60 ml) vegetable oil

1 cup (8 ounces/225 ml) chicken broth

¼ cup (2 ounces/60 ml) light soy sauce

1 pound (450 g) white bread

1 pound 6 ounces (600 g) medium-aged Gouda

2 garlic cloves

4 shallots

2 tablespoons butter

2 tablespoons curry powder

½ cup (4 ounces/125 ml) dry white wine

1 tablespoon cornstarch

2 tablespoons orange juice

Freshly grated nutmeg

Economical

1 Rinse the chicken with cold water, pat dry, and season with salt and pepper. Heat the oil in a skillet and sauté chicken until browned on all sides. Pour in ½ cup (4 ounces/100 ml) of the broth and the soy sauce and cook, covered, over medium heat 10 minutes. Let cool a little and cut into bite-size pieces. Cut the bread into bite-size cubes.

2 Trim crust from the cheese and grate coarsely. Finely chop the garlic and shallots. Melt the butter in a fondue pot (*caquelon*) on the stove over medium heat and sauté the onion and garlic until tender. Stir in curry powder, pour in the remaining broth and the wine, and bring to simmer.

3 Gradually add the cheese, stirring constantly in a figure 8 until melted. Mix the cornstarch with the orange juice, stir into the hot cheese mixture, and bring to simmer again. Season with the nutmeg and pepper and set the fondue on the burner. At the table, spear bread and chicken cubes on fondue forks and draw them through the hot cheese.

Other good accompaniments:

Cooked, shelled and deveined shrimp, small mushrooms, and cooked asparagus tips.

Pour a dry white wine or green tea.

Preparation time: 1½ hrs.
For 6 persons, each portion
about: 765 calories
51 g protein / 37 g fat
55 g carbohydrate

SWEET FONDUES

Dark Chocolate Fondue

1 Rinse dried fruit in a sieve under hot water. Drain and, if necessary, pit. Wash grapes and pull off stems.

2 Wash and dry the pear, quarter, and remove core. Cut quarters crosswise into 1-inch (2-cm) slices. Peel bananas and cut into thick pieces. Immediately toss pear and banana pieces in lemon juice.

3 Cut the cake into bite-size cubes. Arrange decoratively with fruits on a plate.

4 Coarsely chop the chocolate and mix with the milk in the fondue pot (*caquelon*). Melt the chocolate over very low heat on the stove, stirring. Stir in rum if desired. Keep the chocolate mixture hot over a low flame on the burner. At the table, spear fruit and cake on fondue forks and draw through the hot chocolate.

Tips: Children will prefer this fondue without the rum.

Other chocolate varieties are also suitable. Milk chocolate will make the mixture sweeter and milder.

Instead of rum, the fondue can be flavored with orange liqueur and grated orange rind or with almond liqueur and toasted almonds.

Preparation time:
45 min. For 6 persons, each
portion about: 465 calories
7 g protein / 28 g fat
47 g carbohydrate

White Chocolate Fondue

4 to 6 servings

11 ounces (300 g) fresh sour cherries
(or 9 ounces/250 g pitted sour
Morello cherries from a jar)
11 ounces (300 g) sweet cherries (or
9 ounces/250 g pitted dark sweet
cherries from a jar)
¹⁄₄ cup (2 ounces/60 ml) kirsch or
lemon juice
8 ounces (200 g) white chocolate
²⁄₃ cup (5 ounces/150 g) heavy cream
1 vanilla bean
5 ounces (150 g) sugar cookies or
butter cookies

Quick to prepare

1 Wash cherries separately; stem and pit. Place sweet and sour cherries separately in 2 shallow bowls and sprinkle with half of the kirsch. Chill, covered, 30 minutes.

2 Meanwhile, break chocolate in pieces and place in a pot with the cream. Slit vanilla bean lengthwise, scrape out pulp, and add both pulp and bean to chocolate mixture. Melt chocolate over low heat, stirring. Pour mixture into fondue pot (*caquelon*) and place on the burner over a low flame or on a small hot plate.

3 Place cookies in a bowl. Drain cherries and place in serving bowls.

4 Spear 1 sweet and 1 sour cherry on a fondue fork and draw through the hot chocolate. Offer cookies for dipping as well.

Preparation time: 30 min.
(+30 min. marinating time) For
6 persons, each portion about:
410 calories / 4 g protein
24 g fat / 45 g carbohydrate

Tip: This chocolate fondue is guaranteed to be a hit with children if you provide sliced fruits such as pear, kiwi, apples, and peaches on a platter.

Instead of sweet and sour cherries you can dip blue and green grapes.

As an alternative to kirsch, try adding 1½ ounces/40 g/raisins soaked in a few tablespoons of rum just before serving.

4 servings

4 oranges

3 ounces (75 g) amarettini
(tiny amaretti cookies)

3 ounces (75 g) pirouettes
or tuile cookies

4 ounces (100 g) coffee cream-filled
chocolate

1 cup (8 ounces/250 ml) milk

½ cup (4 ounces/125 ml) freshly
brewed espresso

⅔ cup (5 ounces/125 g)
heavy cream

4 teaspoons cornstarch

¼ cup (2 ounces/60 ml) orange
liqueur or orange juice

Easy

Cappuccino Fondue

1 Peel the oranges, removing all white membrane. Cut the sections away from the membranes that separate them, catching the juice. Arrange the sections on a plate. Place amarettini and other cookies in a bowl.

2 Break the chocolate into pieces. Stir all but 3 tablespoons of the milk with the espresso, the cream, and 3 tablespoons of the reserved orange juice in a saucepan and bring to boil, stirring constantly, over low heat. Add the chocolate and let melt, stirring. Mix the reserved milk with the cornstarch and stir in. Simmer 2 to 3 minutes, or until thickened.

3 Transfer the mixture to a fondue pot (*caquelon*) and stir in orange liqueur. Set on a burner over a low flame or on a small hot plate.

4 Spear an orange section on the fondue fork and draw through the chocolate mixture. Serve with the cookies.

Tips: For an even faster fondue, serve sliced banana instead of the oranges.

If some fondue mixture is left over, use it to make an elegant dessert: Fill small individual bowls with balls of vanilla ice cream, pour the hot chocolate cream over, and sprinkle with grated chocolate. Serve immediately.

Variation:
Coffee Chocolate Fondue with Irish Whiskey

Bring 1¼ cups (10 ounces/250 g) heavy cream to boil with 2 teaspoons brown sugar. Coarsely chop 2 ounces (50 g) semisweet chocolate, add to the cream, and let melt, stirring. Mix in 1 cup (8 ounces/250 ml) strong, freshly brewed coffee, reserving 3 tablespoons. Mix the reserved coffee with 4 heaping teaspoons cornstarch, stir into the fondue, and bring to boil. Add ¼ cup (2 ounces/60 ml) Irish whiskey to flavor. Serve with orange sections and cookies as described in the recipe.

Preparation time:
40 min. Each portion about:
550 calories / 8 g protein
32 g fat / 50 g carbohydrate

Chocolate Mint Fondue

4 servings

½ fresh pineapple (1 pound
2 ounces/500 g)
9 ounces (250 g) strawberries
4 ounces (100 g) pound cake
4 ounces (100 g) almond cookies or
sugar cookies
1 cup (8 ounces/200 g)
heavy cream
8 ounces (200 g) peppermint
chocolate
6 fresh mint leaves

Quick to prepare

1 Cut crown from pineapple and remove peel and "eyes." Slice the pineapple, remove core from each slice, and cut the slices in pieces. Wash and hull the strawberries; leave whole or halve. Arrange the pineapple and strawberries decoratively on a platter.

2 Cut the pound cake into bite-size cubes and place in a bowl with the cookies.

3 Heat the cream in a fondue pot (*caquelon*). Break the chocolate into pieces, add to cream, and let melt over low heat, stirring constantly so the mixture does not stick.

4 Set the fondue pot on a burner with a low flame or on a hot plate; keep the chocolate mixture hot but do not boil. Cut mint leaves into fine strips and sprinkle on the fondue.

5 Spear strawberries, pineapple, and pound cake on fondue forks and draw through the chocolate mixture. Serve with cookies.

Special recipe

Surprise the chocolate fans in your circle of friends with a chocolate fondue. It can be quickly prepared and with fresh fruit and cake, it makes a complete meal. If there are no children partaking of the fondue, a shot of peppermint liqueur mixed in just before serving is quite tasty. Tea or coffee is a suitable beverage with the fondue, but a small glass of Prosecco would be welcomed by the adults.

Preparation time: 25 min.
Each portion about:
475 calories / 6 g protein
37 g fat / 39 g carbohydrate

4 servings

2 yeast doughnuts or crullers
1 lemon
2 pounds (800 g) mixed fruit
(strawberries, kiwis, nectarines,
ripe plums, grapes . . .)
1¼ cups (10 ounces/250 g)
whole-milk plain yogurt
1¼ cups (10 ounces/250 g) crème
fraîche or sour cream
4 teaspoons cornstarch
2 tablespoons light honey

Economical

Yogurt Fondue

1 Cut the doughnuts into bite-size pieces. Wash the lemon with hot water and dry. Cut off a piece of the rind and cut into fine strips; finely grate the remaining rind. Squeeze the juice. Clean the fruits and cut into bite-size pieces. Arrange on a plate or in small bowls and sprinkle evenly with lemon juice.

2 In a bowl, stir the yogurt with the crème fraîche and the cornstarch until smooth. Sweeten with the honey and stir in grated lemon rind.

3 Pour mixture into a fondue pot (*caquelon*) and stir over low heat on the stove until smooth and creamy; do not boil. Set mixture on a burner over a low flame and sprinkle with lemon rind strips.

4 Spear doughnuts and fruit on fondue forks and draw through the yogurt mixture.

Preparation time: 40 min.
Each portion about:
460 calories / 7 g protein
30 g fat / 46 g carbohydrate

Sour Cream Fondue

For the Muesli Balls:
2 ounces (50 g) hazelnuts
2 ounces (50 g)
quick-cooking oats
2 ounces (50 g) sesame seeds
3 to 4 tablespoons honey

FOR THE FONDUE:
2 ounces (50 g) seedless raisins
5 tablespoons rum (or apple juice)
5 ounces (150 g) each blue and
green grapes
9 ounces (250 g) strawberries
1 sour apple
1 large banana
Juice and grated rind of ½ lemon
1 package cooked vanilla pudding
1 cup (8 ounces/250 ml) milk
3 tablespoons sugar
1¼ cups (10 ounces/250 g)
heavy cream
10 ounces (250 g) cream cheese

Takes time

1 The day before, for the muesli balls, finely grate the hazelnuts. Toast in a dry skillet with the oats and sesame seeds over medium heat, stirring, until golden brown.

2 Place the mixture in a bowl and work in the honey, using the dough hook on a mixer. Shape walnut-size balls of the mixture, arrange side by side on a plate, and let air dry.

3 For the fondue, rinse the raisins with hot water and soak in rum overnight.

4 The next day, wash and stem grapes. Wash and hull strawberries. Quarter, peel, and core the apple; cut quarters crosswise into pieces. Peel and slice the banana. Immediately sprinkle the apple and banana pieces with 1 to 2 tablespoons lemon juice. Arrange fruit decoratively on a platter.

5 Whisk the pudding powder with 3 tablespoons milk and the sugar in a small bowl. In a saucepan bring the remaining milk and the cream to boil. Remove from heat and stir in the pudding mixture. Quickly bring to boil, then stir in the cream cheese.

6 Transfer the mixture to a fondue pot (*caquelon*) and set on a burner over a low flame or on a hot plate. Stir in the lemon rind, 2 teaspoons lemon juice, and the rum-soaked raisins. At the table, spear muesli balls or fruit on fondue forks and draw through the cream.

Tip from the Pros

It's easiest to shape the sticky muesli mixture by scooping out portions with 2 teaspoons and forming them into balls with dampened hands. If the ball slides off the fondue fork, simply put it on a dessert spoon and dunk it in the creamy sauce. If served chilled, this is a lovely dessert for a hot summer day, for example at a children's backyard party. Refrigerate the sauce until ice cold and set on the table in a bowl. Everyone dips fruit and muesli balls in the same way as for the hot fondue.

Preparation time: 50 min. (+12 hrs. drying and soaking time) For 6 persons, each portion about: 530 calories 12 g protein / 25 g fat / 57 g carbohydrate

4 to 6 servings

10 ounces (250 g) each strawberries, raspberries, and blackberries
4 ounces (100 g) savoiardi (Italian ladyfingers)
4 ounces (100 g) thin European chocolate wafers (for example milk, semisweet, and mocha)
1 pound 2 ounces (500 g) ripe apricots or yellow plums, or 18 ounces (450 g) canned peeled apricot halves
Juice and grated rind of ½ lemon
1 pound 2 ounces (500 g) mascarpone or well-drained cottage cheese
⅓ cup (3 ounces/75 g) powdered sugar
1 packet vanilla sugar
2 teaspoons cornstarch
Wooden skewers

Easy

Apricot Mascarpone Fondue

1 Wash all the berries quickly, drain well, and pick over. Hull the strawberries and halve if necessary. Stick 4 or 5 different berries alternately on wooden skewers. Arrange the skewers on plates.

2 Arrange savoiardi and chocolate wafers on a platter.

3 Pour boiling water over the apricots, rinse with cold water, and peel, then halve and pit (or wash and pit the plums). Chop coarsely, sprinkle with 2 tablespoons lemon juice, and puree in a food processor or with a hand blender.

4 Stir the mascarpone with the powdered sugar, vanilla sugar, and cornstarch in a fondue pot and bring slowly to boil, stirring. Simmer 2 to 3 minutes over low heat, or until the cream is thickened, then gradually fold in the apricot puree. Stir 1 teaspoon grated lemon rind into the cream and bring just to boil.

5 Set the fondue pot on a burner over a very low flame or place on a small hot plate. Draw fruit skewers through the cream. Offer savoiardi and chocolate wafers alongside.

Tip: If you wish, flavor the fondue by stirring in ¼ cup (2 ounces/60 ml) apricot brandy or almond liqueur just before serving.

*Preparation time: 45 min.
For 6 persons, each portion
about: 615 calories
6 g protein / 46 g fat
49 g carbohydrate*

Raspberry Fondue

4 servings

1 small lemon

1 small orange

12 ounces (300 g) fresh or frozen raspberries

1¼ cups (10 ounces/250 g) crème fraîche or sour cream

1 teaspoon vanilla

2 to 3 tablespoons sugar

2 tablespoons raspberry brandy or orange liqueur (optional)

4 ripe but firm peaches

8 ounces (200 g) lemon pound cake

Easy

1 Wash the lemon and orange with hot water and dry. Finely grate the rind of both fruits and squeeze out juice.

2 Wash and pick over the raspberries; puree or press through a sieve. Mix the raspberry puree, lemon and orange juices and rind, and crème fraîche in a fondue pot (*caquelon*). Stir in vanilla, sugar, and brandy or liqueur.

3 Pit the peaches and cut into bite-size cubes. Cut the pound cake into bite-size cubes. Arrange for serving.

4 Warm the raspberry puree on the stove over low heat; do not boil. Set on a burner over a small flame. Spear peaches and cake cubes on fondue forks and draw through the raspberry mixture.

Tip: This fondue is also good made with blackberry puree. Press the berries firmly through a sieve to remove seeds.

Preparation time: 30 min.
Each portion about:
600 calories / 6 g protein
40 g fat / 53 g carbohydrate

4 to 6 servings

For the Chocolate Waffles:

3 tablespoons softened butter
1 tablespoon sugar
Pinch of salt
1 large egg
2 tablespoons cocoa
¾ cup (3 ounces/80 g) all-purpose flour
½ teaspoon baking powder
6 tablespoons milk

FOR THE FONDUE:

2 vanilla beans
2 cups (16 ounces/500 ml) milk
1¼ cups (10 ounces/250 g) heavy cream
2 tablespoons sugar
10 ounces (250 g) strawberries
2 nectarines or peaches
3 tablespoons cornstarch
2 egg yolks

Economical

Vanilla Fondue with Waffles

1 For the chocolate waffles, cream butter with the sugar and salt. Thoroughly blend in the egg. Mix cocoa, flour, and baking powder, sift into creamed mixture, and blend well. Mix in milk. Heat waffle iron and bake the waffle batter. Let cool on a wire rack.

2 For the fondue, slit the vanilla beans lengthwise and scrape out pulp. Combine the vanilla beans and the milk, cream, and sugar in a saucepan. Bring to boil over medium heat, stirring. Let mixture simmer for a few minutes.

3 Hull the strawberries. Quarter and pit the nectarines or peaches; cut the quarters crosswise into thick wedges. Arrange all ingredients decoratively on a platter.

4 Bring fondue back to boil. Stir cornstarch with a little water, pour into fondue, and simmer, stirring, until thickened. Remove the vanilla beans. Whisk egg yolks in a bowl with a few spoonfuls of the vanilla sauce, then stir into the remaining vanilla sauce and pour into a fondue pot (*caquelon*). Set on the burner over a low flame. Spear waffle pieces and fruit on fondue forks and draw through the vanilla fondue.

Preparation time: 45 min.
For 6 persons, each portion
about: 460 calories
8 g protein / 25 g fat
31 g carbohydrate

4 to 6 servings

10 ounces (250 g) strawberries
2 nectarines (about 10 ounces/250 g)
2 to 3 kiwis (about 10 ounces/250 g)
10 ounces (250 g) almond biscotti
1¼ cups (10 ounces/250 g)
heavy cream
2 to 3 teaspoons cornstarch
1¼ cups (10 ounces/250 g) sour
cream or crème fraîche
¼ cup (2 ounces/50 g)
powdered sugar
11 ounces (300 g) ricotta cheese
1 ounce (30 g) unsalted pistachios
½ lemon

Quick to prepare

Ricotta Fondue

1 Clean and hull the strawberries. Halve or quarter if large. Halve and pit the nectarines and cut into wedges. Peel kiwis and cut into eighths. Arrange the fruits and biscotti on a platter.

2 Stir the cornstarch into ¼ cup (2 ounces/60 ml) cream in a small bowl. Mix the remaining cream with the sour cream and powdered sugar in a saucepan and slowly bring to boil over low heat.

3 Stir in the cornstarch mixture and return to boil. Simmer, stirring, until thickened. Gradually whisk in the ricotta and continue whisking until smooth. Pour into a fondue pot (*caquelon*).

4 Chop the pistachios. Finely grate the lemon rind, squeeze juice, and stir both into the ricotta mixture. Set the fondue pot on a burner over a low flame, then stir in the pistachios.

5 Spear fruit pieces on fondue forks and draw through the sauce; dunk biscotti by hand.

Preparation time: 30 min.
For 6 persons, each portion
about: 585 calories
13 g protein / 35 g fat
57 g carbohydrate

Wintertime Citrus Fondue

1 Place the cookies in a bowl. Peel and slice guava; halve slices crosswise. Wash the figs and cut into quarters or eighths. Peel the pear, quarter, core, and cut into pieces; immediately sprinkle with 1 tablespoon lemon juice. Halve the dates lengthwise and pit. Halve the prunes or plums and pit. Arrange all fruits decoratively on a platter.

2 Halve the grapefruits and squeeze out juice; measure 1 cup (8 ounces/250 ml). Beat the egg yolks with the powdered sugar and lemon rind in a metal bowl until thick and creamy. Set the bowl over hot water on low heat and slowly beat in grapefruit juice and remaining lemon juice. Keep beating over water bath until mixture is thick and fluffy.

3 Pour into a fondue pot (*caquelon*) and set on a small hot plate; keep fondue lukewarm. Spear fruit on fondue forks and draw through the fondue. Dunk the cookies by hand. This is very good with espresso or cappuccino.

Tip: If you can find blood oranges, try substituting them for the grapefruits.

Variation:
Fondue with Pomegranate Wine Froth

Halve 2 pomegranates; loosen flesh and seeds with a spoon. Combine with ¼ cup (2 ounces/60 g) sugar and 2 tablespoons water in a saucepan and cook 5 minutes, then press through a fine sieve and stir with 1 tablespoon lime juice and 1 teaspoon grated lime rind. Whisk 4 egg yolks with the pomegranate mixture in a metal bowl until creamy. Set over a hot water bath and beat in ½ cup (4 ounces/125 ml) dry white wine. Heat until mixture is creamy and thick. Serve as described at left.

Coconut Cream Fondue with Tropical Fruit

4 servings
2 ounces (50 g) flaked coconut
4 ounces (100 g) savoiardi (Italian ladyfingers)
$1/2$ ripe mango (10 ounces/250 g)
$1/2$ papaya (10 ounces/250 g)
11 ounces (300 g) fresh pineapple
1 kiwi
2 ounces (50 g) physalis
1 can unsweetened coconut milk (16 ounces/450 g)
$1 1/4$ cups (10 ounces/250 g) heavy cream
$1/2$ cup (4 ounces/125 ml) milk
2 to 3 tablespoons sugar
4 teaspoons cornstarch
1 lime or $1/2$ lemon

Easy

1 Toast the coconut in a dry skillet over medium heat. Place coconut and savoiardi in bowls.

2 Peel the mango, papaya, pineapple, and kiwi. Slice the mango away from the pit. Seed the papaya and cut in wedges. Cut the pineapple in slices and halve them. Cut core from halves, then cut into pieces. Cut kiwi into eighths. Fold the physalis skin back and quickly rinse fruit. Arrange the fruit decoratively on a platter.

3 In a saucepan mix the coconut milk, cream, and all but 3 tablespoons milk and bring slowly to boil. Stir in sugar.

4 Stir the cornstarch into the reserved milk. Stir into saucepan and bring to rolling boil, then reduce heat and simmer uncovered 15 minutes or until the coconut milk is thickened.

5 Finely grate the lime rind and squeeze juice from one half. Stir juice and rind into saucepan. Pour the mixture into a fondue pot (*caquelon*) and set on a burner. At the table, let simmer over low heat. Spear fruit pieces and dip in coconut cream. Roll in coconut flakes, if desired, and accompany with savoiardi.

Tip: If you like, make the fondue more aromatic by adding 2 to 4 tablespoons coconut liqueur.

Preparation time: 45 min.
Each portion about:
545 calories / 6 g protein
30 g fat / 57 g carbohydrate

Children's Surprise Fondue

10 to 12 servings

8 ounces (200 g) white chocolate
1 tablespoon cornstarch
²/₃ cup (5 ounces/150 g) heavy cream
2 cups (16 ounces/500 ml) milk
1 packet vanilla sugar
Pinch of salt
2 ounces (50 g) semisweet chocolate
3 oranges
1 pound 2 ounces (500 g) strawberries
3 to 4 bananas
2 tablespoons lemon juice
6 muffins
5 to 6 soft rolls

Easy

1 Cut the chocolate into small pieces and place in a saucepan. Mix cornstarch with cream. Add milk, vanilla sugar, and salt to chocolate and let melt over low heat, stirring constantly. Stir in cornstarch mixture and bring just to boil. Pour the chocolate fondue into a bowl and let cool. Before serving, sprinkle with the chopped chocolate.

2 Peel the oranges, carefully removing membrane. Divide oranges into sections. Hull strawberries, halving if large. Peel the bananas, cut into thick slices, and sprinkle with lemon juice.

3 Quarter muffins; cut rolls into fairly thick slices. Place the chocolate sauce in the middle of a large platter or tray. Group fruits, muffins, and rolls attractively around it. Have each child spear fruit, muffins, and rolls on a fork and dip them in the chocolate sauce.

Other good dippers:

Apple and pineapple pieces, cherries, prunes, quartered peaches, grapes; small pieces of pound cake, challah, panettone, brioche, or other bread are also suitable if they do not crumble when speared and the pastries are not too sweet.

*Preparation time: 1½ hrs.
For 12 persons, each portion
about: 440 calories
6 g protein / 19 g fat
59 g carbohydrate*

Doughnut Fondue

4 to 6 servings
2¼ cups (9 ounces/250 g) all-purpose flour
2 tablespoons sugar
1 envelope dry yeast
1 cup (8 ounces/250 ml) warm milk
Pinch of salt
1 quart (1 l) vegetable oil for frying
Powdered sugar for sprinkling
For the Berry Sauce:
11 ounces (300 g) frozen mixed berries
2 to 3 tablespoons sugar
3 tablespoons cassis liqueur
1 teaspoon cornstarch
For the Coconut Sauce:
1 cup (8 ounces/200 g) heavy cream
1½ ounces (40 g) flaked coconut
3 tablespoons coconut liqueur or syrup (or 2 to 3 drops coconut extract)
9 ounces (250 g) softened chocolate or vanilla ice cream
Economical

1 For the doughnuts, sift the flour into a bowl. Sprinkle in sugar, scoop a hole in the middle and sprinkle yeast into it. Pour half of the milk into the hole and carefully stir with the yeast. Cover and let rest 30 minutes in a warm place.

2 Add salt, pour in remaining milk, and beat with an electric mixer to form a smooth batter. Let rise, covered, in a warm place, at least one hour.

3 For the berry sauce, mix the frozen berries with the sugar and liqueur in a saucepan and marinate 1 hour. Mix the cornstarch with 2 tablespoons water and stir into the berries. Bring to boil; simmer until sauce thickens. Remove from heat and let cool.

4 For the coconut sauce, bring the cream and flaked coconut to boil. Simmer over medium heat, stirring constantly, 5 minutes, then let cool. Finely puree the coconut sauce in blender, mixing in the coconut liqueur. Just before serving, blend in the ice cream.

5 Heat the oil in a fondue pot and set on a burner. At the table, have diners drop portions of the doughnut batter into the hot oil using a very small ladle or tablespoon. The batter will form irregular shapes. When doughnuts are golden brown, remove with a strainer, drain on paper towels, and dust with powdered sugar. Eat them hot with the cold sauces.

Tip: If children are present, frying in very hot oil should be done by an adult. Hot oil can spatter.

Preparation time: 1½ hrs. (+1½ hrs. resting time) For 6 persons, each portion about: 665 calories / 9 g protein 37 g fat / 61 g carbohydrate

Index

Acknowledgments and Credits

Authors

Petra Casparek

Born and raised in Cologne, Petra Casparek studied folklore as well as Turkish and Middle Eastern history in Munich. She is a freelance journalist who specializes in food and travel and in the folklore of the Middle East and the Arabian Peninsula. On her numerous trips she has collected distinctive recipes and stories about cooking. International dishes are her chief contribution to this book.

Angelika Ilies

Born in Hamburg and now residing near Frankfurt, Angelika Ilies studied ecology, then detoured to London, where she edited for a major publishing house. Upon returning to Germany, she worked in the cooking department of the leading German food magazine. Since 1989 she has been a freelance author and food journalist. Her major contributions to this book are quick and international recipes.

Martina Kittler

After studying ecology and sports, Martina Kittler found her passion in cooking professionally. For eight years she worked on the editorial staff of the leading German food magazine, and since 1991 she has been a freelance food writer. She specializes in healthy cooking with streamlined recipes.

Gudrun Ruschitzka

Born in Saxony, Gudrun Ruschitzka began her career as a cook with a trade publication. After library school and art history studies she worked for an internationally known caterer in Munich. Her specialty is uncomplicated recipes that are adaptable for many guests.

Annette Heisch

Food quality and handling are issues close to Annette Heisch's heart. In 1995, after experience in the test kitchens of a major women's magazine, she turned to freelance journalism and cookbook writing. She contributed marketing information and kitchen techniques to this book.

Photographers

Michael Brauner, Food Photography

After photography school in Berlin, Michael Brauner worked as an assistant to well-known photographers in France and Germany before going off on his own in 1984. His distinctive, atmosphere-rich stills are coveted by numerous advertising agencies and well-known publications.

Teubner Studio and Archives for Food Photography

This studio, established by Christian Teubner in 1962, has enjoyed international prestige. Teubner, a photographer, cook, and gourmet has gained intimate knowledge of ethnic cuisines through numerous trips to every continent. His trademark is exceptionally true-to-life photographic images.

Important Advice

Fondue meals center on an open flame—so be careful that the pot stands firmly on the burner, and do not leave the fondue on the table unwatched, especially if children are in the room. Never add alcohol or other fuel to the burner while the flame is burning or the holder is still hot; always let it cool 5 minutes before refilling. Use special care with an oil fondue. Oil that splashes over can easily flare up. If the fondue should ever catch fire, *do not* douse it with water; instead, smother the fire with a pot lid or other fireproof material. Never heat oil or broth in an earthenware or ceramic pot intended for cheese fondue; the heat can make the ceramic pot crack.

Published originally under the title
—*FONDUE DIE GU KÜCHENBIBLIOTHEK*
© 1998 by Gräfe and Unzer Verlag GmbH, Munchen
English translation © Copyright 2001 by Barron's Educational Series, Inc.
German edition by:
Petra Casparek
Angelika Ilies
Martina Kittler
Gudrun Ruschitzka
Annette Heisch
Photography by Michael Brauner
English translation by Helen Feingold

All inquiries should be addressed to:
Barron's Educational Series, Inc.
250 Wireless Boulevard
Hauppauge, New York 11788
http://www.barronseduc.com

ISBN-13: 978-0-7641-1898-2
ISBN-10: 0-7641-1898-6

Library of Congress Catalog Card No. 00-068877

Library of Congress Cataloging-in-Publication Data
Fondue die GU Küchenbibliothek. English
    Fondue / Petra Casparek . . . [et al.].
        p.   cm.
    Includes index.
    ISBN 0-7641-1898-6
    1. Fondue.   I. Casparek, Petra.
II. Title.
TX825 .F64513 2001
641.8′1—dc21   00-068877

Printed in China
19 18 17 16 15 14 13 12 11

Photo Credits
Title, subtitles, captions, recipe photos, table pg. 8/9, 12/13, kitchen techniques pg. 14, 15, 16 (free space), 18 (heat probe), 19, 20 (free space and chocolate melting) 21 (vegetable defatting), 22, 23 (mortar) and shopping information pg. 28, 30 (vegetables), 31:
Michael Brauner
Table pg. 10/11: stock food Eising
Remaining photographs: Teubner Studio and Archives for Food Photography
Large back cover picture: Uli Franz
Copy: Easy Pic Library Gmb H
Front page: a variation of Vegetarian Fondue with Shrimp (recipe pg. 37)
Back cover: from top to bottom
    Mexican Fondue (recipe pg. 78)
    Chinese Fondue (recipe pg. 53)
    Ricotta Fondue (recipe pg. 135)